From the Library of

Wonderful World of the Bible

THE COURAGEOUS CHRISTIANS

WILLIAM COLEMAN

Designed by Wayne and Rebecca Hanna

Chariot Books is an imprint of David C. Cook Publishing.

THE COURAGEOUS CHRISTIANS
© 1982 William Coleman
Illustration and design by Wayne Hanna, © 1982 David C. Cook Publishing Co.
Printed in the United States of America.

Acknowledgments:
Bible verses are taken from *The Living New Testament,* copyright 1967 by Tyndale House Publishers, Wheaton, Illinois. Used by permission.
Special thanks go to Dr. Gilbert Bilezikian, Professor of Biblical Studies, Wheaton College, Wheaton, Illinois, for serving as this volume's Bible editor.

ISBN: 0-89191-558-3
LC: 81-70519

Contents

An End and a Beginning
Acts 1:3-8

3 During the 40 days after Jesus' crucifixion he had appeared to the apostles from time to time in human form and proved to them in many ways that it was actually he himself they were seeing. And on these occasions he talked to them about the Kingdom of God.

4 In one of these meetings he told them not to leave Jerusalem until the Holy Spirit came upon them in fulfillment of the Father's promise, a matter he had previously discussed with them.

5 "John baptized you with[1] water," he reminded them, "but you shall be baptized with[1] the Holy Spirit in just a few days."

6 And another time when he appeared to them, they asked him, "Lord, are you going to free Israel [from Rome[2]] now and restore us as an independent nation?"

7 "The Father sets those dates," he replied, "and they are not for you to know.

8 "But when the Holy Spirit has come upon you, you will receive power to preach with great effect to the people in Jerusalem, throughout Judea, in Samaria, and to the ends of the earth, about my death and resurrection."

[1] Or, "in."
[2] Implied.

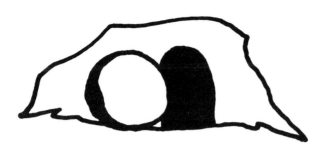

The Happiest People in the World

Can you imagine how you'd feel if your best friend got killed—and then came back to life again? That's just how Jesus' followers felt. They could hardly believe he was really alive—he had to keep proving it to them.

Time for a War?

Now that the disciples knew that death couldn't stop Jesus, they wondered what he would do next. They thought he might lead them into battle against Rome.

Instead, Jesus told them he would send them the Holy Spirit. They knew that meant that he would leave them.

The disciples probably felt confused and a little afraid. They wondered what would happen next.

A Free Israel

The nation of Israel was under Roman rule at this time. Roman soldiers marched in the streets, and a Roman governor ruled the Jews.

The disciples wanted to know if Jesus would set the nation of Israel free.

The Romans destroyed the nation of Israel in A.D. 70. Modern Israel was not established until 1948.

What Is a Holy Ghost?

Instead of saying "Holy Spirit," some Bibles have the older term, "Holy Ghost." The Spirit is not really a ghost as we think of one today, and does not wear a white sheet or make weird noises at night. Jesus had already told the disciples that the Spirit came from God and was a part of God, just as he himself was. The Spirit was an invisible helper who would teach them, comfort them, and give them power.

What Does the Spirit Do?

Can you pick out which jobs the Bible lists as real facts about the Holy Spirit and which ones are phony?

1. Baptizes
2. Gives allowances
3. Makes pizza
4. Comforts
5. Teaches

6. Sings tenor
7. Fills us
8. Changes report cards
9. Appeared as a dove
10. Plays first base

Correct answers:

5: 18. 9. Matthew 3: 16
1. Acts 1: 5. 4. John 14: 26. 5. John 14: 15-17. 7. Ephesians

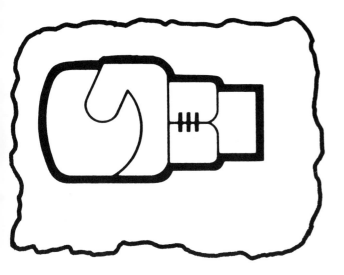

The One-Two Punch

The followers of Jesus were to deliver a message with a one-two punch. They were to tell people about (1) the death and (2) the resurrection of Jesus Christ.

Making Waves

You know what happens when you drop a pebble into a pool of water. The ripples spread out in larger and larger and larger rings from the spot where the pebble went in.

Jesus told his disciples that the message about him should spread in wider and wider and wider circles. See if you can fill in the blanks below, to show where the message was to go.

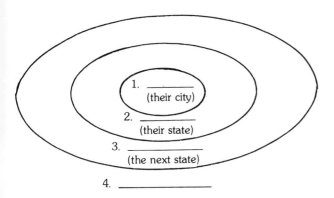

1. _____
   (their city)
2. _____
   (their state)
3. _____
   (the next state)
4. _____

Answers:
1. Jerusalem 2. Judea 3. Samaria 4. The ends of the earth

What Does This Mean to You?

Bubbling Over

"How many of you have ever watched 'The Muppet Show'?" Mrs. Andrews asked the class. Hands shot up and eyes brightened.

"Who's your favorite character?" she continued—and nearly started a battle.

"Miss Piggy!" "Kermit!" "Fozzie Bear!" "Gonzo!" "The Swedish chef!"

The class enjoyed talking about the show, and each person had some reasons ready to show that his or her favorite character was the best one.

The kids in the class were doing for tv characters what Jesus wants his disciples—and us—to do for him. They were talking about someone they liked.

The disciples had plenty to say about Jesus. First of all, they knew Jesus loved them, and that he was the powerful Son of God. They'd seen him die for them and then come back from the dead.

You know the same thing: that the powerful Son of God loves you.

Blast-off!
Acts 1:9-14

9 It was not long afterwards that he rose into the sky and disappeared into a cloud, leaving them staring after him.

10 As they were straining their eyes for another glimpse, suddenly two white-robed men were standing there among them

11 And said, "Men of Galilee, why are you standing here staring at the sky? Jesus has gone away to heaven, and some day, just as he went, he will return!"

12 They were at the Mount of Olives when this happened, so now they walked the half mile back to Jerusalem

13, 14 And held a prayer meeting in an upstairs room of the house where they were staying. Here is the list of those who were present at the meeting: Peter, John, James, Andrew, Philip, Thomas, Bartholomew, Matthew, James (son of Alphaeus), Simon (also called "The Zealot"), Judas (son of James), and the brothers of Jesus. Several women, including Jesus' mother, were also there.

A Super Astronaut

Without the sound of rockets or their red heat and roaring flames, Jesus lifted off the ground. Rising above the Mount of Olives, he soared into the sky.

The disciples stretched their necks and squinted their eyes to watch him as long as they could. Their mouths probably hung open. Suddenly Jesus disappeared into a cloud, and was lost from sight.

Jesus ignored the pull of gravity, the lack of oxygen, and the friction of the atmosphere. The laws of nature could not hinder the Son of God.

Subtraction

Count the number of disciples listed by name in verses 13 and 14. Jesus had originally chosen twelve disciples to follow him and learn from him. How many are missing now? Do you know who?

Answer: Judas Iscariot is missing. After he betrayed Jesus to the men who had him crucified, Judas felt so terrible that he killed himself (*Matthew 27:3-5*). According to Acts 1:26, the eleven disciples elected a man named Matthias to take Judas Iscariot's place.

Good-bye to a Friend

The disciples loved Jesus, and had followed him for three years. They had suffered the agony of watching him be led off to die, and shared the ecstasy of his coming back to life.

Now he was leaving them—in a glorious way, but still leaving. What would they do without him? Jesus had promised to send them the Holy Spirit as a teacher and comforter. But they must have wondered what such a Spirit would be like, and if he could really help them.

The Number One Man

Peter is at the top of the list of disciples in verses 13 and 14, and he later takes a real leadership role in the group. What are his qualifications for leadership?

Education: very little (former fisherman—*Luke 5:3*).

Personality: impulsive (jumped out of boat to meet Jesus walking on the water, then sank halfway there—*Matthew 14:28*).

Loyalty to Jesus: up and down (tried to defend Jesus with a sword when Jesus was arrested; later denied knowing Jesus at all—*John 18:10, Mark 14:66*).

What kind of qualifications are those? Peter certainly wasn't a perfect person. But Jesus had recognized some time earlier that Peter's strong personality could make him a good leader when he used his bravery for God's Kingdom. He said to Peter, "You are Peter, a stone; and upon this rock I will build my church" (*Matthew 16:18*). Now, after making more mistakes and learning from them, Peter became the man the others turned to for leadership.

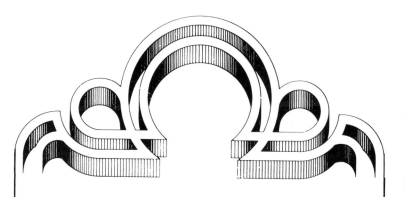

What Does This Mean to You?

We Are Not Alone

How would you like to be two places at once? You could go to the basketball game and still not miss the birthday party John's having. You could go to the school play and still not miss skating at the church social.

Sorry to get your hopes up. You really can't be two places at once. But God can. He can give guidance to an old man in Africa, and in the same moment calm down a frightened child in Chicago. God visits the halls of the White House at the same time that he roams the corridors of your school.

God's ability to be present everywhere guarantees personal attention for us. When we are confused, God promises to be with us, offering comfort and listening. When we face the big decisions at home or school, he is there to guide us.

The early Christians watched the Son of God lift off into heaven. But they knew he hadn't left them alone. They could still pray to God. And Jesus had promised to send the Holy Spirit to be their companion.

God won't leave you. In the living room, locker room, church, bus, playing field, and anywhere, God is there.

Crowns of Fire
Acts 2:1-8, 11, 14-1

2 SEVEN WEEKS[1] HAD now gon by since Jesus' death and resurrection, and the Day of Pentecost[2] arrived. As the believers met together that day

2 Suddenly there was a sound like the roaring of a might windstorm in the skies above them and it filled the house where they were meeting.

3 Then, what looked like flames or tongues of fire appeare and settled on their heads.

4 And everyone present wa filled with the Holy Spirit and began speaking in languages the didn't know,[3] for the Holy Spiri gave them this ability.

5 Many godly Jews were in Jerusalem that day for the religious celebrations, having arrived from many nations.

6 And when they heard the roaring in the sky above the house, crowds came running to see what it was all about, and wer stunned to hear their own languages being spoken by the disciples.

7 "How can this be?" they exclaimed. "For these men are a from Galilee,

8 "And yet we hear them speaking all the native language of the lands where we were bor

. . .

11 "Telling in our own languages about the mighty miracles of God! . . ."

14 Then Peter stepped forward with the eleven apostles and shouted to the crowd, "Listen, all of you, visitors and residents of Jerusalem alike!

15 "Some of you are saying these men are drunk! It isn't true! It's much too early for that! People don't get drunk by 9 a.m.!

16 "No! What you see this morning was predicted centuries ago by the prophet Joel—

17 " 'In the last days,' God said, 'I will pour out my Holy Spirit upon all mankind, and your sons and daughters shall prophesy, and your young men shall see visions, and your old men dream dreams.' "

implied. See Leviticus 23:16.
This annual celebration came 50 days after the Passover ceremonies, when Christ was crucified.
Literally, "in other tongues."

Jerusalem Traffic

More people traveled great distances to Jerusalem for Pentecost than for any other Jewish festival. With Jews there from all over the world, this was a perfect opportunity to teach many people about the resurrection of Jesus Christ.

God's Fire Department

Fire was one of God's favorite ways to appear to people.

He appeared to Moses as a burning bush (*Exodus 3:2*).

He led the Israelites out of Egypt as a pillar of fire at night (*Exodus 13:21*).

He gave the Ten Commandments after appearing in the form of fire (*Exodus 20:18*).

A son of God became the fourth person in the fiery furnace with Shadrach, Meshach, and Abednego (*Daniel 3*).

Flamelike appearances came with the filling of the Holy Spirit (*Acts 2:3*).

What Is a Jew?

Jews weren't just people who spoke in Hebrew. Hundreds of years before Christ, many Jews had been carried off as captives to Babylon and Persia, and had also traveled to other lands: Asia, Egypt, Turkey, Africa, and more. They spoke many different languages, and may have married people from these other lands.

Jews also weren't just people of Jewish ancestry. In the lands they visited, Jews often preached to Gentiles (non-Jews), and converted them to their belief in God and to their Jewish laws.

Was It a Tornado?

Probably not, but it sounded like one. A tornado sounds something like a train would—going through your house!

This noise was so loud that people poured out of their houses to see what was going on.

Shock City

Peter and the other Christians were surprised. They were speaking languages they had not learned. They may have been standing there wide-eyed. One or two might have been holding his throat, afraid of what was coming out. How would you feel if you suddenly began to speak Chinese?

Listeners were no less amazed. They had traveled from far-off countries, and yet they were hearing people speaking their languages.

Time Line

1. How many days after Jesus' crucifixion did he rise into the heavens?
2. How many days after Jesus' crucifixion (which was at Passover time) did the Holy Spirit come upon the disciples? Find the correct places on the time line below.

| Jesus' death | 10 days | 20 days | 30 days | 40 days | 50 days | 60 days |

Answers: 1. 40 days 2. 50 days

Sober as a Stone

Some listeners thought the apostles were merely drunk. However, Peter pointed out that people aren't usually drunk that early in the morning.

Another Promise Kept

The prophet Joel had promised this pouring out of God's Spirit seven hundred years before it actually happened in Acts 2. God keeps his promises—no matter how many years it takes (*Joel 2:28-32*).

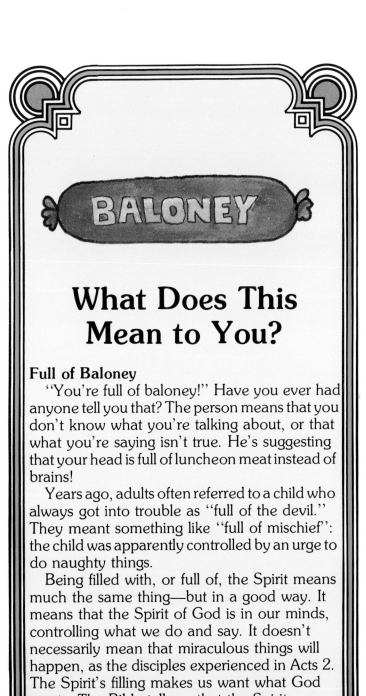

What Does This Mean to You?

Full of Baloney

"You're full of baloney!" Have you ever had anyone tell you that? The person means that you don't know what you're talking about, or that what you're saying isn't true. He's suggesting that your head is full of luncheon meat instead of brains!

Years ago, adults often referred to a child who always got into trouble as "full of the devil." They meant something like "full of mischief": the child was apparently controlled by an urge to do naughty things.

Being filled with, or full of, the Spirit means much the same thing—but in a good way. It means that the Spirit of God is in our minds, controlling what we do and say. It doesn't necessarily mean that miraculous things will happen, as the disciples experienced in Acts 2. The Spirit's filling makes us want what God wants. The Bible tells us that the Spirit encourages love, peace, joy, patience, self-control, and more.

We each choose what we let our lives be filled with—perhaps with the devil, or with baloney, or just with selfishness. The Holy Spirit would like to fill us and give us direction toward the best kind of life.

15

Everything Makes Sense
Acts 2:22-25, 27, 29, 30, 32, 33

22 Peter said, "O men of Israel, listen! God publicly endorsed Jesus of Nazareth by doing tremendous miracles through him, as you well know

23 "But God, following his prearranged plan, let you use t Roman[1] government to nail hi to the cross and murder him.

24 "Then God released hi from the horrors of death and brought him back to life again, f death could not keep this man within its grip.

25 "King David quoted Jes as saying: . . .

27 " 'You will not leave m soul in hell or let the body of yo holy Son decay. . . .'

29 "Dear brothers, think! David wasn't referring to himse when he spoke these words I ha quoted,[2] for he died and was buried, and his tomb is still her among us!

30 "But he was a prophet, and knew God had promised wi an unbreakable oath that one David's own descendants wou [be the Messiah and[2]] sit on David's throne. . . .

32 "He was speaking of Jesus, and we all are witnesses that Jesus rose from the dead.

33 "And now he sits on th throne of highest honor in heaven, next to God. And just promised, the Father has sent th Holy Spirit—with the results yo are seeing and hearing today.'

[1]Literally, "men without the Law." See Romans 2:12.
[2]Implied.

16

THE PALESTINE TRUMPET

published weekly on recycled papyrus ● today's news faster than a speeding chariot ● price: half a shekel

Peter Claims Jesus Is Alive

In an emotional plea Peter, former ringleader in the Jesus movement, claimed today that the Nazarene is alive.

While unable to produce Jesus, Peter nevertheless insisted that he had overcome the grave, and is the long-awaited Messiah.

The speaker seemed to have three reasons to support his theory that Jesus was chosen by God:

1. Jesus performed miracles.
2. Jesus came back from the dead.
3. King David predicted that Jesus would come back from the dead (*Acts 2:22-29*).

These remarks caused a great deal of discussion, but so far no leading Pharisee supports the idea.

Temple in Uproar

Early crowds at the temple were extremely noisy. Some were accused of being drunk.

No arrests were made this morning but several men were accused of public drunkenness as early as 9:00 A.M.

There was much confusion, with a number of people speaking in foreign languages all at once.

A speech by the controversial fisherman, Peter of Galilee, resulted in considerable religious fervor, with a reported three thousand people agreeing to be baptized.

(*Acts 2:40*)

Search for Jesus Continues

After nearly two months of investigation, local authorities seem no closer to finding the missing body of Jesus of Galilee.

Captain Lucius expressed his confidence that the body thieves would soon be apprehended.

Special: Locust Lunch

Covered with honey or olive oil. All you can eat for 1 denarius: Benny's Buffet.

For Sale

One horse and chariot. Good mileage. Horse gets 5 miles to the bale, 6 miles on highway.

Notice:

Chariot races at Pilate Field have been canceled tonight due to religious holidays.

Just What We're Waiting for

The Jews believed that God would someday send them a Messiah, or "Anointed One," who would reestablish Israel as God's kingdom on earth. Many thought this great leader would free them from the Roman Empire (*Acts 1:6*).

Some people today refer to Jewish Christians as "completed Jews." By this they mean that these Jews have found Jesus to be the Messiah that many other Jews are still waiting for.

The Light Goes On

With the Holy Spirit's help, Peter understood how some of the predictions Old Testament writers made about the Messiah fit Jesus.

Positive Proof

Peter pointed out to his audience that when King David said, "You will not . . . let the body of your holy Son decay," he couldn't have been talking about himself. There was proof that David was still dead!

David's tomb was in a part of Jerusalem known as "the City of David" (*1 Kings 2:10*). Many other kings were buried near him.

What Does This Mean to You?

A King's Kid

Have you ever thought of yourself as royalty? Have you ever looked at yourself in the mirror, smiled, and said, "Hello, prince," or "Hello, princess"?

You can, you know. You belong to a royal family if you believe in Jesus. God has started his kingdom of goodness and righteousness on earth. He's promised to banish all evil on some future day.

So you don't have to let that party you didn't get invited to, or that class election you lost get you down for long. You know the king of the universe, and you know that he has plans for the world and for you. You're part of his family.

You're a king's kid!

The World's Biggest Family
Acts 2:41-47

41 Those who believed Peter were baptized—about 3,000 in all!

42 They joined with the other believers in regular attendance at the apostles' teaching sessions and at the Communion services[1] and prayer meetings.

43 A deep sense of awe was on them all, and the apostles did many miracles.

44 And all the believers met together constantly and shared everything with each other,

45 Selling their possessions and dividing with those in need.

46 They worshiped together regularly at the temple each day, met in small groups in homes for Communion, and shared their meals with great joy and thankfulness,

47 Praising God. The whole city was favorable to them, and each day God added to them all who were being saved.

[1]Literally, "the breaking of bread," i.e., "the Lord's Supper."

Love Those Sermons!

Those new believers were really excited. They had just discovered the truth about how God was working in the world. Because they were excited, no one had to urge them to listen to the apostles' sermons—they wanted to learn anything they could about Jesus.

Three Thousand Cousins?

Peter and the other believers felt as close as one big family. They felt a responsibility for each other and wanted to share what they had with one another, especially with those who were poor. Later, a special group of men were assigned to care for the needs of widows *(Acts 6)*.

Some Christians sold all their land. One believer, named Barnabas, sold a field he owned and gave the money to the apostles so they could give it away *(Acts 4:36)*. Others, like Philemon, mentioned later in the New Testament, kept their possessions and used them to serve God. Each did as he felt led of God.

The Word Digger
What Is an Apostle?

The word *apostle* means "someone sent" or "messenger." At first it referred to the original twelve disciples. Later the word was applied to others such as Paul and Barnabas.

Is This Christian Communism?

Definitely not. The believers were practicing Christian sharing, not atheistic communism. There are at least two important differences.

- No believer in the early church was *forced* to surrender his property. Under communism, citizens are forced to share.
- The believers' goal was to show the love of Jesus Christ. Communists want to promote a "fair" way of sharing wealth—but they have no use for a God.

In a Nutshell

Early Christianity attracted the poor.
- Many beggars and handicapped people came to believe in Christ, and needed care.
- Often people lost their jobs when they became Christians, and needed money.
- Later some people were hunted and jailed for believing. Both they and their families needed help with food and other needs.

Brain Drain

Which things does Acts say the early Christians did when they got together? Seven of the choices are correct.

1. Shared everything
2. Gave haircuts
3. Worshiped
4. Ate together
5. Played charades
6. Had Communion
7. Taught
8. Held scavenger hunts
9. Sold pots and pans
10. Prayed
11. Performed miracles
12. Bought magazines
13. Organized a pet shop
14. Sampled yogurt

Answers: 1, 3, 4, 6, 7, 10, 11

No Steeples?

There weren't any church buildings in first-century Jerusalem. Early Christians met in the temple and in synagogues. They also met in private homes.

During later times of persecution they met in many secret places, including some caves. Christians in Rome built secret underground dwellings, called catacombs. The first church buildings were not built until some two hundred years after the chapter you just read.

What Does This Mean to You?

No Solos

When Mary came back from a Christian summer camp, her eyes were sparkling. She had gone horseback riding, ridden over rapids in a canoe, and slept out under the stars. It had been a great two weeks.

However, when Mary talked about her trip with her family, something became obvious. The highlight of camp had been the people there, not the activities.

It had been so neat for Mary to meet girls in her cabin who felt the same way she did about Jesus. They sang songs and prayed together. Mary felt a special closeness to these Christian girls that she didn't feel with her non-Christian friends at school.

And the camp counselor, Deena, had been so warm and caring. Deena's Bible studies were really interesting, too. After camp, Mary got letters from Deena and from some of her other new friends.

As Mary had found, there's something special about friendship with other Christians. We need each other. Christians can share with each other about faith in God, and can encourage each other. They can give each other strength. The believers in Acts seemed to realize this, because they really enjoyed meeting together.

The Christian life is a lot more fun in a group than as a solo act!

A Lame Man Gets a Lift
Acts 3:1-8

3 PETER AND JOHN went to th[e] temple one afternoon to take pa[rt] in the three o'clock daily praye[r] meeting.

2 As they approached the temple, they saw a man lame fro[m] birth carried along the street an[d] laid beside the temple gate—th[e] one called The Beautiful Gate —as was his custom every day.

3 As Peter and John were passing by, he asked them for some money.

4 They looked at him intentl[y] and then Peter said, "Look here!"

5 The lame man looked at them eagerly, expecting a gift.

6 But Peter said, "We don'[t] have any money for you! But I'[ll] give you something else! I command you in the name of Jesus Christ of Nazareth, walk!"

7,8 Then Peter took the lam[e] man by the hand and pulled hi[m] to his feet. And as he did, the man's feet and ankle bones wer[e] healed and strengthened so tha[t] he came up with a leap, stood there a moment and began walking! Then, walking, leaping and praising God, he went into the temple with them.

Think Tank

1. How did the lame man get to the temple?
   Answer: verse 2
2. What did the lame man ask for?
   Answer: verse 3

Some Great Actors

Many beggars walked the streets of Jerusalem or sat along roadsides. Some were really healthy and could have worked—but they preferred to beg because many Jews were so generous! Often these actors would pretend to be blind or limp badly.

The Power of a Name

If you could say "The president sent me on this mission," almost anyone would open his door and let you in. There is great power in the president's name, because anyone who hears it knows the government stands behind that name.

The name of Jesus has *even greater* power:
- We can ask God for things in Jesus' name *(John 14:14)*.
- Demons are cast out in his name *(Luke 9:49)*.
- People are healed in his name *(Acts 3:6)*.
- We can have eternal life through his name *(Acts 4:12)*.

Not Everyone Is Healed

Jesus and his disciples had gone in and out of the temple gates for three years. The lame man had probably been there every day, begging.

Why hadn't someone stopped and healed him before? After three years of ministry by Jesus, there were many lame and blind and deaf in Israel who were not healed. God doesn't heal everyone.

Why not? We can't know the answer to this question entirely, but we have two clues.

First, Jesus and his disciples met a blind man, and the disciples asked if the blindness had come because of something the man or his parents had done wrong. Jesus said, "Neither, . . . but to demonstrate the power of God" *(John 9:3)*. Then he healed the man.

Second, the apostle Paul complained of a physical ailment. We don't know what it was, but we do know that Paul prayed about it three times, and God did not heal him *(2 Corinthians 12:7, 8)*. God explained to him, "I am with you; that is all you need. My power shows up best in weak people" *(2 Corinthians 12:9)*. Paul then was glad to demonstrate Christ's power by enduring his problem.

So this is the answer: Both the blind man, who was healed, and Paul, who wasn't, were to bring honor to God because of what happened.

He Could Have Looked Like a Fool

What would Peter have felt like if he had helped this beggar up—and he wasn't healed? Suppose the beggar struggled to his feet, tottered to the left, and then collapsed in a heap of rags!

Peter knew what it was like to "try" a miracle

and fail. While trying to walk on water, he looked away from Jesus—and then sank *(Matthew 14:28-30)*. On another occasion, he and the other disciples were unable to heal a demon-possessed boy *(Luke 9:40)*.

Peter could have looked like a fool with this lame beggar. He may have had sweaty palms! He must have had great trust in God's power, and confidence that he was doing what God wanted him to do.

What Does This Mean to You?

Modern Miracles

Have you ever thought that God might be too far away in space or too busy to think about you?

Have you ever wondered if God really exists at all? If your prayers go anywhere besides up to the ceiling?

We all wonder such things sometimes. But if we look around ourselves and think a bit, it's not hard to find evidence of God's care. Look at Ann, for example.

The doctor told Ann she had cancer. He said her only hope for life was to have surgery—and even then he couldn't promise success. Naturally, Ann was frightened.

The doctor recommended that Ann have a second round of tests and also get another doctor's opinion. When the second doctor looked at the new test results, he could find no trace of cancer. He could see evidence of it in the first doctor's findings. But now it was gone!

When Ann heard the news, she felt amazed and thankful.

God does many things in our lives to show us he cares. Some things we take for granted, such as getting enough food to eat. Others seem special or miraculous. They all add up to the same thing: God is there, and he cares.

Under Arrest
Acts 4:1-10, 13,18-20

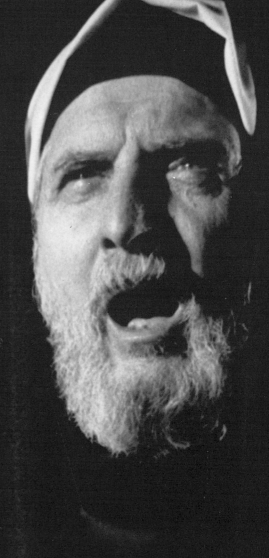

WHILE PETER AND John were ‹ing to the people, the chief ‹ests, the captain of the temple ‹lice, and some of the ‹dducees[1] came over to them,

2 Very disturbed that Peter ‹d John were claiming that Jesus ‹d risen from the dead.

3 They arrested them and ‹ce it was already evening, jailed ‹m overnight.

4 But many of the people ‹o heard their message believed ‹o that the number of believers ‹w reached a new high of about ‹00 men!

5 The next day it happened ‹t the Council of all the Jewish ‹ders was in session in ‹rusalem—

6 Annas the High Priest was there, and Caiaphas, John, Alexander, and others of the High Priest's relatives.

7 So the two disciples were brought in before them. "By what power, or by whose authority have you done this?" the Council demanded.

8 Then Peter, filled with the Holy Spirit, said to them, "Honorable leaders and elders of our nation,

9 "If you mean the good deed done to the cripple, and how he was healed,

10 "Let me clearly state to you and to all the people of Israel that it was done in the name and power of Jesus from Nazareth, the Messiah, the man you crucified—but God raised back to life again. It is by his authority that this man stands here healed! . . ."

13 When the Council saw the boldness of Peter and John, and could see that they were obviously uneducated nonprofessionals, they were amazed and realized what being with Jesus had done for them! . . .

18 So they . . . told them never again to speak about Jesus.

19 But Peter and John replied, "You decide whether God wants us to obey you instead of him!

20 "We cannot stop telling about the wonderful things we saw Jesus do and heard him say."

[1] The Sadducees were a Jewish religious sect that denied the resurrection of the dead.

Trouble

When the disciples preached that Jesus had come back from the dead, they got into trouble—in this case, with the Sadducees (SAD-ja-sees). The Sadducees were a religious party that did not believe in the resurrection of anyone.

Unable to accept most supernatural events, the Sadducees didn't believe God would send a Messiah or interfere in this world. Every time they heard someone say that Jesus came back from the dead they seemed to get a gigantic headache.

The Pharisees *did* believe in resurrections and *were* looking for a Messiah—but Jesus wasn't the type they had in mind. They were probably glad he was dead.

Numbers Rising

About 120 believers were left after Jesus rose into heaven *(Acts 1:15)*. On the graph below, find how many people believed in Jesus (1) after Peter's first sermon, and (2) after the miracle in the temple (total number).

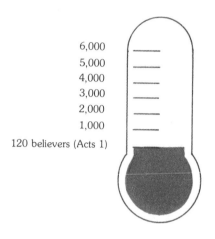

6,000
5,000
4,000
3,000
2,000
1,000
120 believers (Acts 1)

Answer: (1) 3,000 (2) 5,000

Flashback

The prediction by Jesus came true. He had said that his followers would go to prison for their faith *(Luke 21:12)*.

The Lid Popped Off

The priest Caiaphas (KAY-uh-fass) had had Jesus arrested and executed in order to put a lid on his followers. But a few months later the lid was popping off—Christianity was spreading into the thousands! Caiaphas was still fighting hard to tie the lid on the situation.

Check It Out

They Didn't Like Miracles

When Jesus brought Lazarus back from the dead, his religious enemies wanted to hide the evidence—by killing Lazarus! The miracles of Jesus were so obvious it drove his enemies goofy *(John 12:10)*. These people were now having the same difficulty with Peter's miracles.

Deep Trouble

The Supreme Court of Jerusalem in those days was called the Sanhedrin or the Council. It consisted of seventy men, plus the High Priest. They had full authority over religious matters in Israel as well as over some civil and criminal matters.

The Council Peter and John faced was the same Council that had tried Jesus and condemned him.

Dummies!

The Council had its prejudices, and they were not about to listen to these men. They called Peter and John "uneducated" (verse 13). They used the Greek word *idios*, from which we get *idiot*.

Peter and John had Galilean accents (Matthew 26:73) and Galileans were considered crude and rude.

They also had no advanced training in the Jewish laws. They had hauled fishnets, not studied. The Council members had known this about them before.

Since the Council did not want to believe in Jesus' resurrection anyway, it was easy for them to dismiss these men as empty-headed.

No Teeth Chattering

Even though their lives were in danger, these courageous Christians refused to back down. The Bible mentions their boldness three times (verses 13, 29, and 31). Peter had acted like a coward when Jesus was crucified, and he never wanted to let his beloved Master down again.

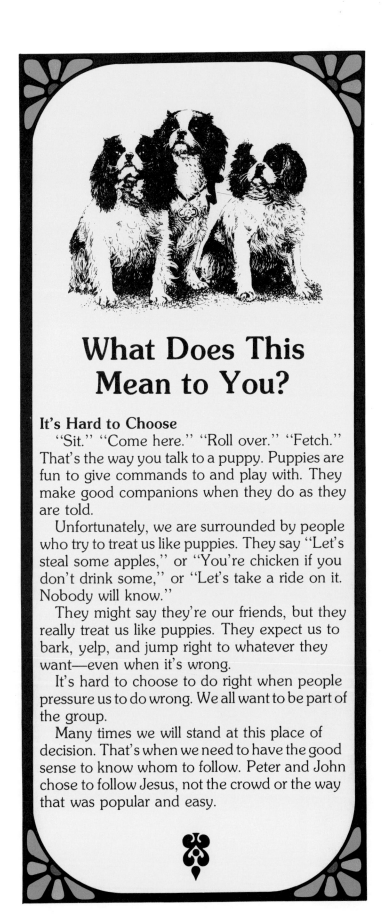

What Does This Mean to You?

It's Hard to Choose

"Sit." "Come here." "Roll over." "Fetch." That's the way you talk to a puppy. Puppies are fun to give commands to and play with. They make good companions when they do as they are told.

Unfortunately, we are surrounded by people who try to treat us like puppies. They say "Let's steal some apples," or "You're chicken if you don't drink some," or "Let's take a ride on it. Nobody will know."

They might say they're our friends, but they really treat us like puppies. They expect us to bark, yelp, and jump right to whatever they want—even when it's wrong.

It's hard to choose to do right when people pressure us to do wrong. We all want to be part of the group.

Many times we will stand at this place of decision. That's when we need to have the good sense to know whom to follow. Peter and John chose to follow Jesus, not the crowd or the way that was popular and easy.

A Clever Cover-up
Acts 4:37—5:11

37 Barnabas was one of those who sold a field he owne and brought the money to the apostles for distribution to those i need.

BUT THERE WAS a man
ned Ananias (with his wife
phira) who sold some
perty,
  And brought only part of
money, claiming it was the full
e. (His wife had agreed to this
eption.)
  But Peter said, "Ananias,
an has filled your heart. When
u claimed this was the full price,
u were lying to the Holy Spirit.
  "The property was yours to
 or not, as you wished. And
r selling it, it was yours to
cide how much to give. How
uld you do a thing like this? You
ren't lying to us, but to God."
5 As soon as Ananias heard
se words he fell to the floor,
ad! Everyone was terrified,
5 And the younger men
vered him with a sheet and took
 out and buried him.
7 About three hours later his
e came in, not knowing what
d happened.
3 Peter asked her, "Did you
ople sell your land for such and
h a price?" "Yes," she replied,
e did."
9 And Peter said, "How
uld you and your husband even
nk of doing a thing like
s—conspiring together to test
 Spirit of God's ability to know
at is going on?[1] Just outside
t door are the young men who
ried your husband, and they
l carry you out too."
10 Instantly she fell to the
or, dead, and the young men
me in and, seeing that she was
ad, carried her out and buried
r beside her husband.
11 Terror gripped the entire
urch and all others who heard
at had happened.

rally, "to try the Spirit of the Lord."

Hard to Figure Out

Ananias and Sapphira (Sa-FIRE-ah) wanted to look more "religious" than they really were. They were not forced to sell their property, but chose to. They wanted to look as good as Barnabas had.

Then, in order to impress everyone with their generosity, they claimed they had contributed *all* the money they had received from the sale. In fact, they only gave part of it. By claiming to give it all they had hoped to impress everyone.

God wasn't impressed.

Sherlock the Apostle

How did Peter figure out that Ananias was lying? We don't know. Probably the Holy Spirit guided him to the secret.

The Ax Falls

Peter didn't strike Ananias dead. In fact, he may have been surprised when God did. Why did it happen?

Apparently God didn't want anyone destroying the reputation of the believers, or lowering their standards. God started the church with very strict rules.

After the death of these two, all the believers were terrified, and checked themselves to see if they were doing things that were dishonest. They knew that they could not use belief in Jesus as a cover-up to hide crooked lives.

Same-Day Service

It was a Jewish custom to bury a person the same day he died. Some Jews keep this same practice today.

Fill 'Er Up

Earlier descriptions of the believers (*Acts 2:4; 4:8*) mention that they were "filled with the Spirit."

Peter told Ananias that Satan had filled his heart. The problem with Ananias and Sapphira was that they allowed Satan to take control of them (*verse 3*).

Job Description

There are certain jobs Satan does particularly well. He likes to:
- tempt people (*Matthew 4:3*)
- deceive them (*Revelation 12:9*)
- lie (*John 8:44*)
- murder (*John 8:44*)
- accuse (*Revelation 12:10*)
- destroy (*Revelation 9:11*)

He is such a despicable character that he is called the "ancient serpent" (*Revelation 12:9*).

Puzzling

This is a rebus riddle, in which the placement of the letters, words, or pictures adds up to make a phrase. This rebus riddle will tell you *when* Sapphira went to see the apostles.

Ananias   R R R

Answer: Three "hours" after Ananias.

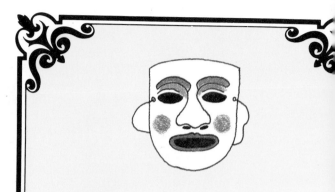

What Does This Mean to You?

Halloween Masks All Year?

Have you ever noticed yourself wearing a mask to school? I don't mean the kind of mask you tie on with a string, but an invisible mask. You're wearing a mask when you act as if you really don't care about that friend who didn't invite you to his party—even though you're really hurting inside. You wear a mask when you act tough and cool to impress certain kids, talking about cheating and smoking and shoplifting as if you approve of such things.

Some people wear masks to church. They try to look very religious on Sundays, just to impress other people. Inside they really aren't interested in pleasing God at all.

Ananias and Sapphira wanted everyone to think they were very generous. They acted as if they were giving all the money they'd made by selling some land, while they were really holding much of it back. It wasn't wrong for them to give only a certain amount of money to God. But it was wrong for them to lie about it.

It's much better to be honest. There's no need to put up a big front. God loves us and accepts us in spite of all our weaknesses and failures. He can also deal with our problems much better if we're honest with him about them.

Doesn't it feel good to know we don't have to pretend?

scape!

cts 5:12, 17-22, 25-29, 33-35, 39

12 Meanwhile, the apostles re meeting regularly at the mple in the area known as lomon's Hall, and they did any remarkable miracles among e people. . . .

17 The High Priest and his atives and friends among the dducees reacted with violent lousy

18 And arrested the apostles, d put them in the public jail.

19 But an angel of the Lord me at night, opened the gates of e jail and brought them out. en he told them,

20 "Go over to the temple d preach about this life!"

21 They arrived at the temple out daybreak, and immediately gan preaching! Later that orning[1] the High Priest and his courtiers arrived at the temple, and, convening the Jewish Council and the entire Senate, they sent for the apostles to be brought for trial.

22 But when the police arrived at the jail, the men weren't there. . . .

25 Then someone arrived with the news that the men they had jailed were out in the temple, preaching to the people!

26, 27 The police captain[2] went with his officers and arrested them (without violence, for they were afraid the people would kill them if they roughed up the disciples) and brought them in before the Council.

28 "Didn't we tell you never again to preach about this Jesus?" the High Priest demanded. "And instead you have filled all Jerusalem with your teaching and intend to bring the blame for this man's death on us!"

29 But Peter and the apostles replied, "We must obey God rather than men. . . ."

33 At this, the Council was furious, and decided to kill them.

34 But one of their members, a Pharisee named Gamaliel, . . .

35 Addressed his colleagues as follows: "My advice is, leave these men alone. If what they teach and do is merely on their own, it will soon be overthrown. . .

39 "But if it is of God, you will not be able to stop them, lest you find yourselves fighting even against God."

[1]Implied.
[2]Literally, "the captain of the temple."

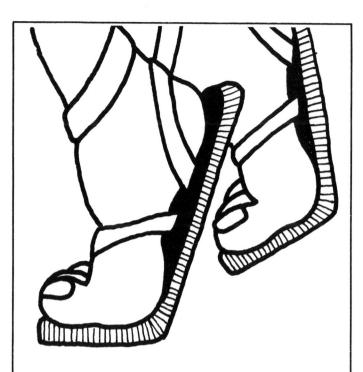

Tiptoed

If the angel had chosen, the apostles could have walked *through* the gate. Jesus once came through a door *(John 20:26)*.

But this time they just quietly opened the locked gate, reclosed it, and smoothly tiptoed past the guards without being seen.

What Do You Think?

Did the angels make the apostles invisible?
Did they sneak quietly past?
Did the angel put a spell on the guards so they could not see?
Pick the one that sounds best to you.

Who's Who?

It looks like all twelve of the apostles were thrown into the cooler this time *(verses 18, 29)*.

Job Description

The police captain was in charge of the temple police. Their job was to maintain order in the temple, keep it clean, keep unlawful visitors out, and patrol the area at night.

They were also on call for the Sadducees to use.

A Hot Job

If the police captain found a policeman asleep on the job, he could set the napper's clothes on fire.

Brain Thumpers

1. When did the angel come?
   Answer: verse 19
2. When did the apostles arrive back at the temple?
   Answer: verse 21
3. Was the jail door unlocked?
   Answer: verse 23
4. Why did the police treat the apostles gently?
   Answer: verses 26, 27

Nice Police

The Bible teaches us to obey the police *(Romans 13:3)*. We need them. Police and other authorities are servants from God given for our protection and safety.

Very seldom have Christians had to decide to disobey the police. But sometimes police or governments have urged Christians either to do wrong things, or not to worship God. When that happens, God must come first *(Acts 5:29)*.

Word Picture

One of the apostles' enemies was the

_____ .

Answer:
High Priest

A Cool Head

One member of the Council kept control of his temper. Gamaliel's cool head saved the apostles' lives. He pointed out that if the apostles were doing something God didn't like, God would take care of them. On his advice, the Council let the apostles go.

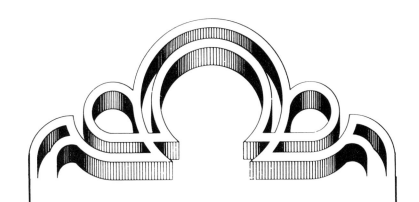

What Does This Mean to You?

Faith on the Firing Line

Persecution doesn't happen just to gray-haired adults or to people in far countries. Christian young people in America often suffer in certain ways because of their faith. Have any of these happened to you?

Rick earned the nickname "Reverend Rick" because he attended a Christian group at his school. He kept going to it anyway.

Wendy was laughed at because she refused to sneak into a ball game without paying. She wouldn't let a little laughter change her standards.

Kristi was called names because she was a friend to a girl from a foreign country. She decided to ignore the ridicule.

Most of us have never been threatened with jail because of our faith, as the apostles were. But we have felt pressure. That is when we have to decide if we are going to obey God or man.

The First Victim
Acts 6:8, 9, 11, 12; 7:1-2, 51-60

7 THEN THE HIGH Priest asked him, "Are these accusations true?"

2 Stephen's reply was lengthy. . . .

51 "You stiff-necked heathen! Must you forever resist the Holy Spirit? But your fathers did, and so do you!

52 "Name one prophet your ancestors didn't persecute! They even killed the ones who predicted the coming of the Righteous One—the Messiah whom you betrayed and murdered.

53 "Yes, and you deliberately destroyed God's Laws, though you received them from the hands of angels."[3]

54 The Jewish leaders were stung to fury by Stephen's accusation, and ground their teeth in rage.

55 But Stephen, full of the Holy Spirit, gazed steadily upward into heaven and saw the glory of God and Jesus standing at God's right hand.

56 And he told them, "Look, I see the heavens opened and Jesus the Messiah[4] standing beside God, at his right hand!"

57 And they mobbed him, putting their hands over their ears, and drowning out his voice with their shouts,

58 And dragged him out of the city to stone him. The official witnesses—the executioners—took off their coats and laid them at the feet of a young man named Paul.[5]

59 And as the murderous stones came hurtling at him, Stephen prayed, "Lord Jesus, receive my spirit."

60 And he fell to his knees, shouting, "Lord, don't charge them with this sin!" and with that, he died.

8 Stephen, the man so full of faith and the Holy Spirit's power,[1] did spectacular miracles among the people.

9 But one day some of the men from the Jewish cult of "The Freedmen" . . .

11 Brought in some men to lie about him, claiming they had heard Stephen curse Moses, and even God.

12 This accusation roused the crowds to fury against Stephen, and the Jewish leaders[2] arrested him and brought him before the Council. . . .

[1]Literally, "full of grace and power."
[2]Literally, "the elders and the Scribes."
[3]Literally, "the Law as it was ordained by angels."
[4]Literally, "the Son of Man."
[5]Paul is also known as Saul.

Double Insult

What would you call someone who refused to listen? Bullheaded? Dense? Stubborn?

A favorite Jewish term was "stiff-necked." God started it: he called the Jews stiff-necked when they continued to disobey him while they were wandering in the wilderness (*Exodus 33:5*).

"Heathen" is one of the worst names anyone can call a group of religious people. It means they are irreligious.

Stephen used both these terms. He was blunt in denouncing the disobedience of the Jews. He was a great deal like John the Baptist—his honesty got him into trouble.

Risky Business

Not many life insurance companies would sell policies to prophets. They were too often in danger.

- Isaiah was probably sawed to pieces.
- John the Baptist's head was cut off (*Matthew 14:10*).
- Jeremiah was jailed (*Jeremiah 37:15; 38:6*).
- Queen Jezebel killed many prophets, and tried to kill Elijah (*1 Kings 19:1-3; 18:3, 4*).

The people who killed Stephen did not actually kill other prophets. But they were guilty of having the same narrow thinking as those who had done so.

A Real Nice Guy

It seems that Stephen was a very special person. He was one of seven men chosen by the apostles to help care for Greek-speaking widows among the believers. The writer of Acts twice singles Stephen out of those seven as being "unusually full of faith and the Holy Spirit" (*Acts 6:5, 8*). He was smart and a good speaker, judging by the talk he gave to the Council at his trial. (You only see the end of the speech here.) God used him to do many amazing miracles (*Acts 6:8*).

Get the Picture?

Stephen said about the worst thing he could have. He told the Council he saw Jesus standing by the right hand of God.

The Council had condemned Jesus as an impostor and fool. Stephen told them they had killed the wrong man, for Jesus was really the Son of God.

Not many people could have shown the courage Stephen had! While surrounded by a hostile crowd, he told them exactly what they did not want to hear.

Did You Know?

Whoever testified against a person had to throw the first stone at his execution (*Deuteronomy 17:7*).

Stones were used because they were the most plentiful weapons in Israel.

This must have been a miserable way to die, since stoning might not kill the victim quickly.

Angry leaders on one occasion picked up stones and threatened to stone Jesus (*John 10:31*).

Close-up

More than a Mob

The angry crowd was careful to follow the exact rules set down in Old Testament law for execution by stoning. They didn't just lose their tempers: they did some deliberate planning.

- They took Stephen outside the city (*Leviticus 24:13, 14*).
- More than one witness was present.
- A witness threw the first stone (*Deuteronomy 17:5-7*).

Rebus Puzzle

Stephen had a _____ attitude toward those who killed him.

Answer: ɓuᴉʌᴉɓɹoɟ

A Big Waste?

Why did God allow Stephen to be killed? Peter and the other believers may have wondered that. God had saved Peter's life a couple of times already, after all. And Stephen showed such promise! It might have seemed like a big waste. The believers probably felt both sad and afraid.

But Jesus had not promised his followers that their lives would be easy. He said that the world would hate them as it had hated him (*John 15:18, 19*). But he promised to be with them always (*Matthew 28:20*).

And though God didn't stop the cruel killing of Stephen, he brought something good out of it. In the persecution that followed Stephen's death, the believers scattered—and took the good news of Jesus with them to new places (*Acts 8:1*).

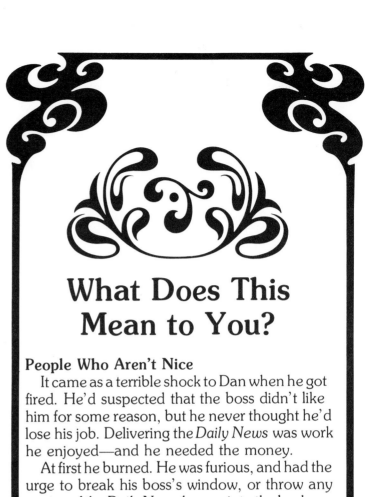

What Does This Mean to You?

People Who Aren't Nice

It came as a terrible shock to Dan when he got fired. He'd suspected that the boss didn't like him for some reason, but he never thought he'd lose his job. Delivering the *Daily News* was work he enjoyed—and he needed the money.

At first he burned. He was furious, and had the urge to break his boss's window, or throw any copies of the *Daily News* he saw into the bushes.

But after a while, Dan settled down. He knew that there was no sense in getting even. That would be mean and wrong.

It was hard, but a week later, Dan forgave his grouchy boss. He even waved at him when he saw him on the street.

It's easy to forgive nice people. They probably won't bother you again. The tough task is to forgive someone like Dan's boss, who was not so nice.

Knowing what Jesus said on the cross helped Dan a great deal. If Jesus could forgive the people who were killing him, then he could give Dan the strength needed to forgive an unfair boss.

Stephen probably didn't see any friendly smiles on the faces of those who were stoning him. Yet he asked God to forgive them anyway.

The Church Goes Underground
Acts 8:1-6

8 PAUL WAS IN complete agreement with the killing of Stephen. And a great wave of persecution of the believers bega. that day, sweeping over the church in Jerusalem, and everyone except the apostles fle into Judea and Samaria.

2 (But some godly Jews[1] came and with great sorrow buried Stephen.)

3 Paul was like a wild man, going everywhere to devastate the believers, even entering private homes and dragging ou men and women alike and jailin them.

4 But the believers[2] who ha fled Jerusalem went everywher preaching the Good News abou Jesus!

5 Philip, for instance, went t the city of Samaria and told the people there about Christ.

6 Crowds listened intently t what he had to say because of th miracles he did.

[1] Literally, "Devout men." It is not clear whether these were Christians who braved the persecution, or whether they were god and sympathetic Jews.
[2] Literally, "the church."

38

Paul Acted Crazy

Luke says Paul attacked Christians as savagely as a wild beast tears at a victim's body.

Paul received special permission from the Council to hurt Christians (Acts 26:10).

As part of his persecution, Paul tortured Christians (Acts 26:11).

Paul would even chase men and women out of their homes (Acts 8:3).

His prisoners were often locked in chains (Acts 9:2).

Interestingly, Paul had gotten his education from Gamaliel (Acts 22:3, 4), the man who had convinced the Council not to kill the apostles. Evidently Paul didn't agree with his former teacher about how to treat Christians.

Profile

The Number One Christian-hunter

Birthplace: Tarsus in Cilicia, a Roman province (now in Turkey). Because Paul was born there, he was automatically a Roman citizen.

Nationality: Jewish, of the tribe of Benjamin. Paul's family was probably part of a large Jewish community in Tarsus, and may have moved to Jerusalem when Paul was young.

Education: Paul's family thought highly enough of Jewish law—and of Paul's ability to learn it—to send him to study under the famous Gamaliel.

Personality: Apparently very strong-willed about what he believed!

Archenemies

If Peter and Paul had ever met at this point, they might have considered each other archenemies.

Peter was the leader of the group Paul wanted to wipe out. Paul was the number one Christian-hunter. Each believed strongly that he was right and the other was wrong.

Even if they'd had similar beliefs, they might not have gotten along very easily. Paul was well-educated and well-traveled. Peter had only been a fisherman in Galilee. They had very different backgrounds.

Spreading the Fire

The enemies of the Christians thought they could break up the group by scattering it. But that was like trying to put out a fire by throwing each burning log onto a different pile of hay! Everyplace the believers went, they told about Jesus, and more people believed in him.

Samaria, Samaria

Like New York City in New York state, Samaria was the name of a city in a region which was also called Samaria.

A Danger Zone

The hate between Jews and Samaritans always made it a danger zone. Jews were never sure how they might be treated around Samaria.

Jesus made a peaceful stop there (John 4). Later he recommended that his disciples stay clear of the area (Matthew 10:5). Just before he went into heaven Jesus told his followers to preach there again (Acts 1:8).

Pack Your Bags

If you thought that half the town wanted to kill you because you were a Christian, what would you do? Would you take just a few clothes and run for your life? Would you move everything you owned in a moving van? Would you leave in the middle of the night, or wear a disguise? Where would you go?

The believers in Jerusalem had to think about all these things.

Hitting the Road

Many people traveled in New Testament times. Fairly passable roads twisted through Palestine, and great roads crisscrossed the rest of the Roman Empire. Some of the Romans' better highways are still used today.

Most people traveled by walking. Some carried extra sandals as we carry spare tires. Others rode on horses or donkeys or used ox wagons and horse-drawn carts.

Ships were another good way to get around, but sometimes pirates and storms made sailing treacherous.

In spite of the slow pace of transportation, travelers made long trips during this time. It would have been possible for the scattered Christians from Jerusalem to have gone as far as China, Russia, Scandinavia, and central Africa.

What Does This Mean to You?

A Good Deal Out of a Bad Deal

As far as Angie was concerned, moving was the worst thing that had ever happened to her. She really liked her old school and had a good set of friends there.

It seemed unfair. Her parents had made the decision to move, and now she was stuck with it! For a while Angie sulked and a couple of times cried.

When she got to the new city Angie was surprised to find two terrific friends right away. Soon she was involved in the school volleyball team, and things began to look up.

After a while Angie had to admit it to herself: she was better off after the move than she had been before.

God has promised to work good out of bad situations in his children's lives *(Romans 8:28)*. The persecution of Christians was terrible. Many were arrested, and some executed. Yet God worked it out for good: thousands of people heard about Christ because of the evil persecution.

imon's Magic Show
cts 8:9-14, 17, 18, 20, 22-24

9, 10, 11 A man named Simon had formerly been a sorcerer in Samaria for many years; he was a very influential, proud man because of the amazing things he could do—in fact, the Samaritan people often spoke of him as the Messiah.[1]

12 But now they believed Philip's message that Jesus was the Messiah, and his words concerning the kingdom of God; and many men and women were baptized.

13 Then Simon himself believed and was baptized and began following Philip wherever he went, and was amazed by the miracles he did.

14 When the apostles back in Jerusalem heard that the people of Samaria had accepted God's message, they sent down Peter and John. . . .

17 Then Peter and John laid their hands upon these believers, and they received the Holy Spirit.

18 When Simon saw this —that the Holy Spirit was given when the apostles placed their hands upon peoples' heads—he offered money to buy this power.
. . .

20 But Peter replied, "Your money perish with you for thinking God's gift can be bought!
. . .

22 "Turn from this great wickedness and pray. Perhaps God will yet forgive your evil thoughts—

23 "For I can see that there is jealousy[2] and sin in your heart."

24 "Pray for me," Simon exclaimed, "that these terrible things won't happen to me."

[1]Literally, "this man is that Power of God which is called great."
[2]Literally, "the gall of bitterness."

Do You Believe in Magic?

When we talk about magic today, we usually mean "magic tricks"—tricks that fool the audience. The magician is clever enough to make it look as if he has amazing power—power to pull a rabbit out of an empty hat or to find a certain card in a deck without looking. All he really has is clever fingers.

The other kind of magic is the kind which depends on the power of evil spirits to do these amazing things. The Bible forbids the practice of this second kind of magic *(Deuteronomy 18:9-14)*.

Magician School

The Egyptians had schools to train their magicians. Their textbooks were called "The House of Life."

When he graduated, a magician was expected to recite from memory every spell for each situation.

A Lucky Bowl

Sometimes an ancient family would keep a wooden bowl in their home, with sayings written all over it. These sayings were supposed to ask good spirits to keep evil spirits away.

Rat Radar

Some magicians listened to the noises made by rats and watched their behavior. Certain cries and movements were supposed to tell the magician the future.

Black and White Magic

Black magic is the kind that brings evil to people, such as curses. White magic is supposed to cause something good. Simon probably practiced white magic. He did it so well that many people believed he was sent from God *(verse 11)*. But he probably used evil powers to do these deeds, just so people would admire him.

Sale! Used Crutches Cheap

Almost every place they went, the apostles were performing miracles *(Acts 2:43)*.

Lame people were jumping in the air *(Acts 3:7, 8)*. Buildings shook *(Acts 4:31)*. Jail gates swung open *(Acts 5:19)*.

Mind Transplant

John had visited Samaria once before with Jesus. He didn't like Samaritans much: they were of a different race, and didn't get along with the Jews.

When the people did not listen to Jesus' message, John angrily asked him to pour down fire from heaven and burn the Samaritans up (Luke 9:54).

Now God had changed the way John thought. He hurried to the city of Samaria to help the new believers. God performs some great thinking transplants.

Pick a Pair

Two of these pairs are true and two are not. Can you pick the correct pair of pears?

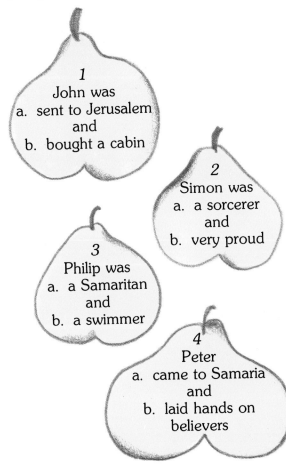

1
John was
a. sent to Jerusalem
and
b. bought a cabin

2
Simon was
a. a sorcerer
and
b. very proud

3
Philip was
a. a Samaritan
and
b. a swimmer

4
Peter
a. came to Samaria
and
b. laid hands on believers

Answer: The correct pear pair is 2 and 4.

What Does This Mean to You?

Witches and Spells

The magic tricks you see at parties and talent shows can usually be explained. And if you read a book about magic tricks, and practice them, you can probably do some "magic" yourself, such as making a coin disappear. A recent magazine story explained how magicians make it look as if they are sawing people in half, when they really aren't.

The problem with magic comes when a person starts looking for *real* power to perform amazing feats—power from the supernatural, from spirit beings. He may be entering an area where Satan has control.

Supernatural power can only come from two sources: either from God, or from Satan and his demons.

Some people, like Peter and the other apostles, pray for God to show his power, in order that people might worship him.

Others, like Simon, are only interested in power for power's sake. Simon liked to impress people. He made a good target for Satan, who could tempt him with a little power—and then take control of him. The Bible warns us to stay away from the evil kind of magic and leave it alone (Deuteronomy 18:9-14).

Philip's Chariot Ride
Acts 8: 26-32, 35-40

26 An angel of the Lord said to Philip, "Go over to the road that runs from Jerusalem through the Gaza Desert, arriving around noon."

27 So he did, and who should be coming down the road but the Treasurer of Ethiopia, a eunuch of great authority under Candace the queen. He had gone to Jerusalem to worship at the temple,

28 And was now returning in his chariot, reading aloud from the book of the prophet Isaiah.

29 The Holy Spirit said to Philip, "Go over and walk along beside the chariot!"

30 Philip ran over and heard what he was reading and asked, "Do you understand it?"

31 "Of course not!" the man replied. "How can I when there is no one to instruct me?" And he begged Philip to come up into the chariot and sit with him!

32 The passage of Scripture he had been reading from was this: "He was led as a sheep to the slaughter, and as a lamb is silent before the shearers, so he opened not his mouth. . . ."

35 So Philip began with this same Scripture and then used many others to tell him about Jesus.

36 As they rode along, they came to a small body of water, and the eunuch said, "Look! Water! Why can't I be baptized?"

37 "You can," Philip answered, "if you believe with all your heart." And the eunuch replied, "I believe that Jesus Christ is the Son of God."

38 He stopped the chariot, and they went down into the water and Philip baptized him.

39 And when they came up out of the water, the Spirit of the Lord caught away Philip, and the eunuch never saw him again, but went on his way rejoicing.

40 Meanwhile, Philip discovered himself at Azotus!

Under the Magnifying Glass

- *Candace* was not the name but the title of the Ethiopian ruler, like *Pharaoh* or *Caesar*.
- What the Bible calls Ethiopia is not modern Ethiopia, but was what is now southern Egypt and northern Sudan.

Word Worker

The Ethiopian may have been the kind of person called a *proselyte*. A proselyte was a non-Jew who was converted to Judaism, and followed the Jewish laws and customs in every way.

Compact Car

The Ethiopian's chariot was apparently the transportation type instead of the war model. It was carrying only a couple of passengers, and probably was drawn by one or two horses.

Carriages were made of wood and leather with metal fittings. The wheels had six to eight spokes each. Since owning a chariot was a mark of wealth and power, Philip may never have ridden in one before.

We aren't sure how many miles the horse traveled to a bucket of feed.

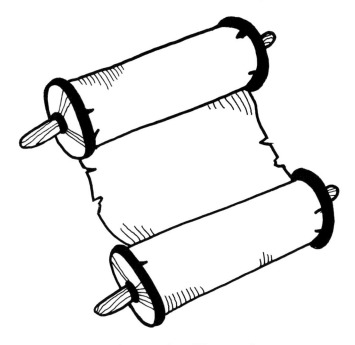

Paperback Books

The Ethiopian was reading the Book of Isaiah, but what he held did not look like our books. Called a scroll, it was made of leather, papyrus, or parchment sheets. This book was one wide page rolled up rather than many pages attached at one edge.

Scrolls were usually one foot wide and up to 35 feet long. Many scrolls rolled on two large rods that looked like rolling pins.

The entire Book of Isaiah could fit on one scroll.

Hebrew is read from right to left instead of left to right, the way we read English.

Some Words about Water

When Jesus had left the disciples, he asked them to gather followers for his kingdom, and baptize them, and teach them *(Matthew 28:19)*. Christians today do not all agree on how to baptize, but all feel it is important to obey Jesus' command.

Every new believer in Acts was baptized.

No Crystal Ball

The eunuch was reading Isaiah 53, and asked Philip who Isaiah was talking about. Philip knew immediately that the prophet was writing about Jesus.

Isaiah knew how Jesus was going to die. He described the trial and death around seven hundred years before it happened.

Since he was a prophet of God, he could predict some things about the future. And he didn't need a crystal ball.

A Rebus Quiz

What word in the story of Philip and the Ethiopian does this picture make you think of?

Answer: This is a chariot (cherry-it).

Rocket Exit

When the job was over, Philip disappeared in a second. We don't know how the Spirit moved Philip, but he was suddenly gone. He found himself in Azotus, 25 miles away.

What Does This Mean to You?

Feeling Important

How do you feel about yourself? On some days do you think you're as useless as roller skates on a whale? Do you feel as dumb as a square tire? All of us wonder sometimes if we're worth anything.

That's when we need to be reminded how important we are in God's eyes. You aren't a number lost on a busy street, or a face melting in a huge crowd. You are more than a zip code, a phone number, a locker number, and a seat assignment.

You are a person. And God is busy watching over and caring about your life, with all its ups and downs.

Can you imagine how special the Ethiopian must have felt? God sent one person across the desert just to meet him. God must have loved that Ethiopian a lot. Just the way he loves you.

ireworks for Paul
cts 9:1-9

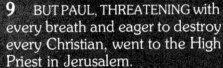

9 BUT PAUL, THREATENING with every breath and eager to destroy every Christian, went to the High Priest in Jerusalem.

2 He requested a letter addressed to synagogues in Damascus, requiring their cooperation in the persecution of any believers he found there, both men and women, so that he could bring them in chains to Jerusalem.

3 As he was nearing Damascus on this mission, suddenly a brilliant light from heaven spotted down upon him!

4 He fell to the ground and heard a voice saying to him, "Paul! Paul! Why are you persecuting me?"

5 "Who is speaking, sir?" Paul asked. And the voice replied, "I am Jesus, the one you are persecuting!

6 "Now get up and go into the city and await my further instructions."

7 The men with Paul stood speechless with surprise, for they heard the sound of someone's voice but saw no one!

8, 9 As Paul picked himself up off the ground, he found that he was blind. He had to be led into Damascus and was there three days, blind, going without food and water all that time.

Shower of Light

A strange light suddenly flooded Paul as he was walking down the road. The light was special for several reasons:

- It came from heaven. *(Acts 9:3)*
- It was at noon. *(Acts 22:6)*
- It was brighter than the sun. *(Acts 26:13)*
- It left Paul blind. *(Acts 9:8)*

Maybe the light spread across the sky like a huge fireworks show. Or it could have come down like a giant spotlight beam.

Confusion Corner

Many of us have two names. You might be both James and Jim, or both Elizabeth and Beth.

Paul also had two names. When he played with his Jewish friends he was Saul. However, his Greek-speaking friends always threw the ball to Paul. His name didn't change; he had both.

Dragon Breath

The persecution after Stephen's death was so harsh that most Christians escaped from Jerusalem *(Acts 8:4)*. Their flight did not satisfy the enraged Paul. He followed them to Damascus, 150 miles from Jerusalem, in order to bring them to trial. His every breath was filled with hate for Christians *(verse 1)*. If he could have, he might have breathed real fire.

Pestering Jesus

When someone is persecuted it means he is harassed, hurt, or even killed.

The person who persecutes or picks on Christians is really hurting Jesus Christ. That is what Jesus told his disciples *(Luke 10:16)*. And that is what he now told Paul *(Acts 9:5)*, the chief persecutor.

Actions Louder than Words

The Bible doesn't record Paul as saying, "Jesus, I believe in you now," or anything like that. But Paul obeyed what Jesus told him: he went on to Damascus and waited for instructions.

Opinion Polls

1. Why do you think Paul hated Christians?
2. Why didn't Jesus strike Paul dead?
3. Why did Paul come to obey Jesus?

The Missing Three

For three days Paul went without three things. What were they?

Answer: sight, food, and water.

Just for Fun

See if you can answer these riddles:
1. How do we know the light from heaven was intelligent?
2. What did Paul fall into?

Answers: 1. It was brilliant. 2. A trance.

What Does This Mean to You?

The Big Decision

When pop singer B.J. Thomas became a Christian, he made a dramatic turnaround. After ten years on drugs he could see a tremendous change in his life.

With Paul the same was true. He had hated the church badly enough to kill—until he met Jesus Christ for himself, in a burst of light and glory.

For most of us it was a little calmer when we became Christians. And we almost envy people like B.J. Our lives might seem like big bores in comparison with the dramatic work God did in his life.

But we shouldn't feel that way. Every conversion is spectacular. A great battle went on inside you when you finally decided that you wanted God to control your life. A great transplant happened, and you received a new, God-powered kind of life that will last forever.

If you accepted Christ as you knelt by your bed, that's stupendous. If you did it at church, your conversion is outstanding. There are no big conversions and little ones. Yours is as great a miracle as any in the world.

A Double Agent?
Acts 9: 10-13, 15, 17-20, 23-27

10 Now there was in Damascus a believer named Ananias. The Lord spoke to him in a vision, calling, "Ananias!" "Yes, Lord!" he replied.

11 And the Lord said, "Go over to Straight Street and find the house of a man named Judas and ask there for Paul of Tarsus. He is praying to me right now, for

12 "I have shown him a vision of a man named Ananias coming in and laying his hands on him so that he can see again!"

13 "But Lord," exclaimed Ananias, "I have heard about the terrible things this man has done to the believers in Jerusalem! . . ."

15 But the Lord said, "Go and do what I say. For Paul is my chosen instrument. . . ."

17 So Ananias went over and found Paul and laid his hands on him.

18 Instantly (it was as though scales fell from his eyes) Paul could see, and was immediately baptized.

19 Then he ate and was strengthened. He stayed with the believers in Damascus for a few days

20 And went at once to the synagogue to tell everyone there the Good News about Jesus— that he is indeed the Son of God!
. . .

23 After a while the Jewish leaders determined to kill him.

24 But Paul was told about their plans, that they were watching the gates of the city day and night prepared to murder him.

25 So during the night some of his converts let him down in a basket through an opening in the city wall!

26 Upon arrival in Jerusalem he tried to meet with the believers, but they were all afraid of him. They thought he was faking!

27 Then Barnabas brought him to the apostles and told them how Paul had seen the Lord on the way to Damascus, what the Lord had said to him, and all about his powerful preaching in the name of Jesus.

Two Ananiases

You're right! The Damascus believer God spoke to in verse 10 had the same name as the man who lied to the apostles *(Acts 5:1, 2)*.

Ananias would have been happy if God had given this assignment to someone else. Paul had a terrible reputation for arresting Christians.

It was just as if God asked you to deliver a ham sandwich to the house of a famous murderer. You might swallow hard before you agreed to go.

It's Still There

Little has changed in Damascus since the time of Paul. One street is called "Straight." It might be the exact one where Ananias met Paul.

Did Paul Have Scales?

Probably not. Paul had been blinded by the bright light when Jesus appeared to him *(Acts 9:8, 9)*. When he received his eyesight, it was as sudden as if dry fish scales were falling off his eyeballs.

A Sneaky Spy?

The Christians had plenty of reason to distrust Paul *(verse 21)*. He would have done anything to wreck Christianity and arrest believers *(Acts 9:1)*. The disciples had been hurt badly by this man and did not want to fall into a sneaky trap.

Elevator Service

Paul didn't leave town by the same kind of elevator that you might see in downtown Chicago, but the basket elevator got the job done.

There were many baskets around large enough to hold a man. They were often used to carry wool, hay, or straw.

Wall Houses

Some houses were actually built into the walls of a city. The windows were often high in the wall. Paul must have escaped from one of these.

A Little Too Exciting

It looked like Paul couldn't win. He had just become a Christian and already five groups were furious at him:

- Christians in Damascus didn't trust him (verse 21).
- Jewish leaders wanted to kill him (verse 23).
- The Damascus government wanted to arrest him (2 Corinthians 11:32).
- Christians in Jerusalem thought he was faking (verse 26).
- Greek-speaking Jews planned to murder him (verse 29).

All of this, and he had been a Christian for only three days! He must have found the Christian life exciting.

Some Bright Spots

Paul had plenty of enemies, but not everyone was nasty to him. Can you name three persons or groups from this passage who helped Paul?

Answers: Ananias, Barnabas, and the people who helped Paul escape Damascus.

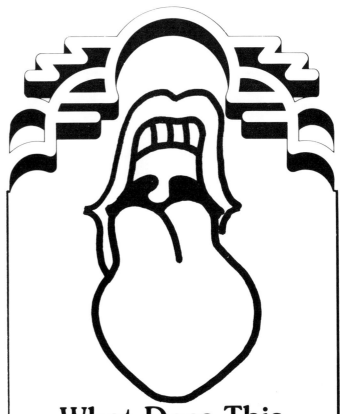

What Does This Mean to You?

Taking a Chance

Brett can be a nice person sometimes, but he also has a lot of rough edges. The jokes he tells are so off-color they could make steel warp. Often his language is strong enough to make a sailor blush.

Yet Sandy continues to be his friend. She knows Brett is a new Christian. Beneath his rough manners and garbage mouth there is a person who trusts Jesus.

When Brett goes wrong, Sandy gently points it out. When other kids walk away, she stays around. She is taking a chance on him. Sandy trusts God to be able to change Brett, and she wants to help it happen.

Barnabas would understand that kind of trust. It's the same type he gave to Paul—even though Paul didn't seem to deserve it.

She Wouldn't Stay Dead
Acts 9:36-43

36 In the city of Joppa the was a woman named Dorcas ("Gazelle"), a believer who wa always doing kind things for others, especially for the poor.

37 About this time she became ill and died. Her frienc prepared her for burial and lai her in an upstairs room.

38 But when they learned that Peter was nearby at Lydd they sent two men to beg him return with them to Joppa.

39 This he did; as soon as h arrived, they took him upstairs where Dorcas lay. The room wa filled with weeping widows whe were showing one another the coats and other garments Dorc had made for them.

40 But Peter asked them all leave the room; then he knelt ar prayed. Turning to the body h said, "Get up, Dorcas,"[1] and sh opened her eyes! And when sh saw Peter, she sat up!

41 He gave her his hand an helped her up and called in the believers and widows, presentir her to them!

42 The news raced through the town, and many believed ir the Lord.

43 And Peter stayed a long time in Joppa, living with Simor the tanner.

[1]Literally, "Tabitha," her name in Hebrew.

The Disciple Was a Lady

Dorcas is the only woman in the Bible who is called a disciple in the original Greek language. However, she wasn't the only lady to act like one by showing faith and loyalty to Jesus.

From the very beginning, ladies played a large role in the early church:

- Mary, the mother of Jesus, and other women prayed in the upper room with the apostles (Acts 1:14).
- The Holy Spirit enabled women to prophesy (Acts 2:17).
- Women went to jail for their faith (Acts 8:3).
- Philip had four daughters who served as preachers (Acts 21:9).
- Mary, Mark's mother, used her home to house Peter in spite of the danger (Acts 12:12).
- Lydia, the businesswoman, opened her home to the apostles (Acts 16:15).
- Priscilla taught Apollos, in order to make his ministry complete and more useful (Acts 18:26).

Beautiful Eyes

Dorcas is the Greek word for gazelle. Gazelles are small, graceful antelopes noted for their beautiful eyes. Maybe Dorcas did have a lovely look—gazelles were often symbols of beauty.

Bone Needles

Men were not too proud to sew in Bible times. Paul used a needle to make his living sewing tents (Acts 18:3). Dorcas put her skills to work making clothes for her friends and for widows. Needles in those times were not made from steel but from bronze or splinters of bone.

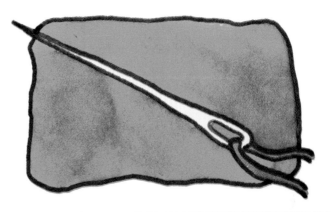

Professional Weepers

At a Jewish funeral, the mourners did not sob gently. In most cases they cried loudly, and often beat themselves on the chest.

At most funerals, at least two flute players and one professional weeper were hired.

We don't know if Dorcas's funeral had professional weepers. We do know that she had many friends who cried sincerely over her.

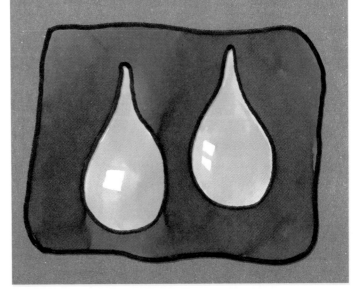

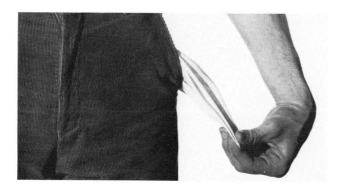

Jesus Loved Empty Pockets

Dorcas loved the poor just as Jesus had before her. Christ told his followers to give to the poor *(Matthew 19:21)*. He also wanted believers to invite the needy to have dinner with them *(Luke 14:13,14)*.

Often the early Christians took offerings for the poor *(Romans 15:26)*.

As a believer Dorcas was willing to do what she could to help, giving her time and energy.

Hold Your Nose

As a tanner, Simon's work was to make animal hides into leather—and it was a stinking job. He soaked the skins in lime and sometimes treated them with dog dung. Often tanners had to live outside of town because of the terrible smell of their work.

If a Jewish woman married a man and later discovered he was a tanner, she could legally divorce him!

Peter must have had a strong stomach to stay in the house of Simon the tanner *(verse 43)*.

What Does This Mean to You?

Sharing Friendship

Connie was going through the sack of clothes in the living room to see what her family was giving to the Laotian refugees their church was helping. She was surprised to find two pairs of jeans that were practically brand-new.

"Don't these jeans fit you?" Connie asked her sister Denise.

"Sure, they fit," Denise answered. "But I have four pairs, and Sompan doesn't have any."

Denise cared about her new Laotian friend, Sompan. She knew that Sompan had had to leave everything behind—including her parents—when she fled from the Communists in her homeland. And Denise knew that caring meant sharing.

Caring for someone means more than just saying "Hi" and talking about the weather. Caring also means more than just giving someone a toy you used years ago, or clothes you don't like. Sometimes the sharing involved in caring might hurt a little. It might mean sharing something precious to you: time or money or possessions.

It takes a lot of courage to be able to give. What if you are sorry later? What if you need those things or that money tomorrow?

It can be hard. But because Jesus wants us to care and share, he can help us do so.

10 IN CAESAREA THERE lived a Roman army officer, Cornelius, a captain of an Italian regiment.

2 He was a godly man, deeply reverent, as was his entire household. He gave generously to charity and was a man of prayer.

3 While wide awake one afternoon he had a vision—it was about three o'clock—and in this vision he saw an angel of God coming toward him. "Cornelius!" the angel said.

4 Cornelius stared at him in terror. "What do you want, sir?" he asked the angel. And the angel replied, "Your prayers and charities have not gone unnoticed by God!

5, 6 "Now send some men to

Joppa to find a man named Simon Peter, who is staying with Simon, the tanner, down by the shore, and ask him to come and visit you. . . ."

9, 10 The next day, Peter went up on the flat roof of his house to pray. It was noon and he was hungry, but while lunch was being prepared, he fell into a trance.

11 He saw the sky open, and a great canvas sheet,[1] suspended by its four corners, settle to the ground.

12 In the sheet were all sorts of animals, snakes, and birds [forbidden to the Jews for food[2]].

13 Then a voice said to him, "Go kill and eat any of them you wish."

14 "Never, Lord," Peter declared, "I have never in all my life eaten such creatures, for they are forbidden by our Jewish laws."

15 The voice spoke again, "Don't contradict God! If he says something is kosher, then it is! . . ."

17 Peter was very perplexed. What could the vision mean? What was he supposed to do? Just then the men sent by Cornelius had found the house and were standing outside at the gate. . . .

23 So Peter invited them in and lodged them overnight. The next day he went with them to Caesarea, accompanied by some other believers from Joppa. . . .

28 Peter told Cornelius, "You know it is against the Jewish laws for me to come into a Gentile home like this. But God has shown me in a vision that I should never think of anyone as inferior."[3]

[1]Implied.
[2]Implied; see Leviticus 11 for the forbidden list.
[3]Literally, "that I should not call any man common or unclean."

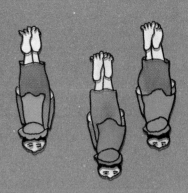

The Day It Rained Corneliuses

In 80 B.C. the Roman Empire became packed with Corneliuses when a man named Cornelius Sulla freed ten thousand slaves—and named each of them after himself! The Cornelius in this chapter may have been a descendant of those former slaves.

A Big Cheese

Name: Cornelius
Job title: Captain or centurion
Army served: Roman Empire
Number under command: 100 Italian volunteers
Religious interest: Gentile who loved God

Knocking Heads

So far all the Christians had been Jews—or else non-Jewish proselytes, like the Ethiopian, who completely followed Jewish laws and customs. People like Cornelius presented problems. Cornelius believed in God, but had not tried to keep all the Jewish laws. Could such a person follow Jesus without first becoming fully Jewish?

God seemed to answer "Yes" to that question during Peter's visit, because he sent the Holy Spirit to Cornelius and others present. But the problem still caused a big argument during a church council later.

Don't Eat Bat Burgers

God had told Moses to list many animals, birds, and reptiles that Jews could not eat. They included eagles, mice, snails, lizards, storks, and sea gulls. Also, the Jews were not allowed to eat pigs or camels *(Leviticus 11:13-30)*.

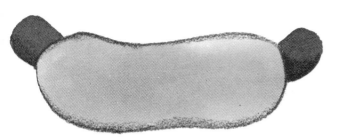

Hot Dogs, Etc.

What does *kosher* mean? It is a Hebrew word meaning proper, fit, or good. The voice told Peter that everything he saw on the sheet was good to eat.

You can still buy kosher foods, such as kosher hot dogs, in many grocery stores today. These foods have been prepared according to the ancient Jewish dietary laws, and are mainly purchased by Jews who follow these laws today.

2 + 2 = 4

Peter put two and two together. God had set down a life-style for the Jews as his special, chosen people, and forbidden them to eat certain foods. Now, in the vision to Peter, God said these foods were OK.

When Peter heard that a Roman named Cornelius wanted to see him, he understood what God was telling him. Though the Jews had always considered the Gentiles unfit to be included in God's promises (just as some foods were unfit to eat), now Peter knew the Gentiles were part of God's planned kingdom.

What Does This Mean to You?

Invisible Walls

Debbie was a new girl at church. And because she wasn't the outgoing type, and was a little on the chubby side, it was easy for the other kids to simply pass her by.

The kids in the church were busy with their own activities. They were used to each other. It was fun to go places together and enjoy their own group. They didn't need anybody new.

Each week Debbie came to church, and inside she hoped. Too shy to reach into the group, she hoped they would reach out and welcome her. But when two months went by and nothing happened, Debbie was ready to give up.

Closed-up cliques aren't what God wants. He wants his love in us to cross the walls that separate us, to get past labels like "pretty" or "ugly," "burn-outs" and "jocks," blacks and whites, poor and rich, American and Iranian and Mexican and Vietnamese.

When Peter found out that God wanted him to cross the invisible wall between Jews and Gentiles, he did so right away. God loves all people, and we should too.

Coach Barnabas
Acts 11:19-22, 24-26

19 Meanwhile, the believe[rs] who fled from Jerusalem duri[ng] the persecution after Stephen['s] death traveled as far as Phoeni[cia] Cyprus, and Antioch, scatterin[g] the Good News, but only to Je[ws]

20 However, some of the believers who went to Antioc[h] from Cyprus and Cyrene also gave their message about the Lord Jesus to some Greeks.

21 And the Lord honored t[he] effort so that large numbers o[f] these Gentiles became believe[rs]

22 When the church at Jerusalem heard what had happened, they sent Barnabas [to] Antioch to help the new conve[rts]
. . .

24 Barnabas was a kindly person, full of the Holy Spirit a[nd] strong in faith. As a result larg[e] numbers of people were added [to] the Lord.

25 Then Barnabas went on [to] Tarsus to hunt for Paul.

26 When he found him, h[e] brought him back to Antioch; a[nd] both of them stayed there for a f[ull] year, teaching the many new converts. (It was there at Antio[ch] that the believers were first call[ed] "Christians.")

A Truckload of Antiochs

The Greek King Seleucus loved his father Antiochus so much he named sixteen cities Antioch (AN-tee-ock). This Antioch in Syria, built in 301 B.C., became the third largest city in the Roman Empire. With a population of five hundred thousand, it was about the size of Pittsburgh or Atlanta.

The Fourth Circle

In Acts 1: 8, Jesus had told his disciples to take his message to Jerusalem (their city), Judea (their state), Samaria (the next state), and the ends of the earth. By telling people in Phoenicia, Cyprus, and Antioch about Jesus, the Christians had reached the outer circle. But the effort to make sure the message gets to all people in every part of the earth still goes on today.

A Nice Nickname

Can you figure out the name this rebus puzzle stands for?

His real name was Joseph, but the apostles nicknamed him Barnabas, meaning "Preacher" or "Encourager" *(Acts 4: 36)*. He earned his name because he was a bighearted Christian.

Barnabas Goes Hunting

When Barnabas saw Gentiles flocking to Jesus Christ, he knew he would need help. His mind turned to an old friend. He had not seen Paul for years (maybe ten years) but he was determined to find him.

The hunt was hard because Paul had gone into hiding when certain Jews tried to kill him. Eventually they got together and Barnabas and Paul ministered in Antioch for one year.

A Mystery

What had Paul been doing between his first visit to the apostles in Jerusalem and the time Barnabas found him?

No one knows. It may have been during that time that Paul had his vision of heaven *(I Corinthians 12: 1-4)*.

What would you guess he was doing, knowing Paul?

Sharp as a Tack

1. The church at Jerusalem sent Barnabas to help
   a. find Paul.
   b. make new converts.
   c. run a bake sale.
2. Where did Barnabas go to find Paul?
   a. Antioch.
   b. The Yellow Pages.
   c. Tarsus.
3. Antioch was the first place believers were called
   a. Christians.
   b. disciples.
   c. Presbyterians.

Answers: 1. b 2. c 3. a

Super Barnabas

Look, it's an apostle! No, it's a friend! No, it's a missionary! No, it's Super-Barnabas!

These are a few of the fantastic things this bighearted apostle did:

- Sold his field and gave the money to the needy (Acts 4:37).
- Became Paul's friend when other apostles didn't trust him (Acts 9:26, 27).
- Helped start first Gentile church when others didn't trust Gentiles (Acts 11:22).
- Took food to starving Christians in Jerusalem (Acts 11:27-30).
- Befriended a young man named Mark when Paul didn't trust him (Acts 15:39).

A New Nickname

Christians probably did not choose to call themselves Christians. People around Antioch began calling them that. "There go the followers of Christ" is what they were saying. Some may have said the word as an insult. Others probably used it with admiration.

Early Christians were also called "The Way," disciples, believers, saints, and brothers.

What Does This Mean to You?

Becoming an Octopus

If you are ever grabbed by an undersea creature and wonder what has captured you, just hold your breath and count arms. If you count eight, you've met an octopus!

The octopus's eight arms are useful for reaching out. And at the time of history you just read about, the church of Jesus Christ was beginning to look like an octopus. It was reaching out in many directions, to many new places. Many different individuals helped the church move out.

Christians today continue to reach out to new places and new people, and the church is still growing new arms. It would certainly be impossible for this to happen if just one person did the work and everyone else sat around. That person would get discouraged, and maybe give up.

But if we all help, by living as Jesus wants us to, and telling others about Jesus, the church will keep growing.

You can't be the whole octopus. But the church needs you to be one arm.

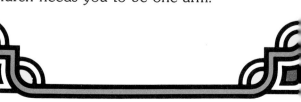

isit from a Ghost?

cts 12:1-10, 12-16

ABOUT THAT TIME King rod moved against some of the ievers,

And killed the apostle[1] nes (John's brother).

When Herod saw how ch this pleased the Jewish ders, he arrested Peter during Passover celebration

And imprisoned him, cing him under the guard of 16 diers. Herod's intention was to ver Peter to the Jews for cution after the Passover.

But earnest prayer was going up to God from the church for his safety all the time he was in prison.

6 The night before he was to be executed, he was asleep, double-chained between two soldiers with others standing guard before the prison gate,

7 When suddenly there was a light in the cell and an angel of the Lord stood beside Peter! The angel slapped him on the side to awaken him and said, "Quick! Get up!" And the chains fell off his wrists!

8 Then the angel told him, "Get dressed and put on your shoes." And he did. "Now put on your coat and follow me!" the angel ordered.

9 So Peter left the cell, following the angel. But all the time he thought it was a dream or vision, and didn't believe it was really happening.

10 They passed the first and second cell blocks and came to the iron gate to the street, and this opened to them of its own accord! So they passed through and walked along together for a block, and then the angel left him. . . .

12 After a little thought Peter went to the home of Mary, mother of John Mark, where many were gathered for a prayer meeting.

13 He knocked at the door in the gate, and a girl named Rhoda came to open it.

14 When she recognized Peter's voice, she was so overjoyed that she ran back inside to tell everyone that Peter was standing outside in the street!

15 They didn't believe her. "You're out of your mind," they said. When she insisted they decided, "It must be his angel. [They must have killed him.[2]]"

16 Meanwhile Peter continued knocking! When they finally went out and opened the door, their surprise knew no bounds.

[1]Implied.
[2]Implied.

Can You Remember?

James is the second of Jesus' original twelve disciples to die. Can you remember who the first one was?

Answer: Judas Iscariot

Not That James

The James who was executed was a disciple and the brother of John. The James mentioned later in Acts is the half brother of Jesus. Later, this James became a leader in the church *(Acts 15)*.

First Automatic Doors?

As Peter walked through the prison, the iron gate leading to the street opened automatically —long before the electric eye was invented *(verse 10)*.

Guards Are Carted Off

When Herod discovered that Peter had escaped, he had sixteen guards arrested. They were punished by the ruthless king.

Later, under the Code of Justinian, when a prisoner got away the guards could be forced to carry out the prisoner's punishment. All sixteen of Peter's guards may have been executed because he got away.

Hotheaded Herods

The Herod family was a group of bloodthirsty rulers whom Rome allowed to govern the Jews.

- Herod the Great murdered children in Bethlehem *(Matthew 2)*.
- Herod Antipas beheaded John the Baptist *(Mark 6:14-28)*.
- Herod Agrippa I had James executed *(Acts 12)*.
- Herod Agrippa II tried Paul for being a Christian *(Acts 26)*.

Angelic Miracle Act

Peter got to see one of the great miracle acts of all time. The fisherman was so amazed that he thought he was dreaming.

ZAP: A light flooded the cell.

ZAP: An angel appeared.

ZAP: Chains fell off.

ZAP: The iron gate swung open.

Puzzled Peter

The apostle was left standing in the cold. Rhoda was so surprised to see Peter that she forgot to let him in.

He must have scratched his head with one hand while he knocked again with the other. If they were so thrilled to see him, they could at least open the door!

Fellowship of Fugitives

As the Christians prayed for Peter they may also have spent considerable time praying for themselves.

It was extremely dangerous to be a Christian. One of their leaders had been executed, and another faced the same fate.

At any minute soldiers might break down their door and arrest them all.

What Does This Mean to You?

Expecting the Best

Do you have any friends who are always upbeat? They expect good things to happen. These people can be fun to be around.

Other people are glum and expect everything to go wrong. They start to become a drag.

This is where the Christian can have a definite advantage. He shouldn't be glum about a problem. He can ask God to help him and then begin to hope for a good result.

A Christian shouldn't pray for a safe trip and then expect an accident. He shouldn't pray for a clear mind to take an exam and then resign himself to flunking. A believer shouldn't talk to God about an argument with a friend, and then avoid the person because of fear that things won't clear up.

The early Christians prayed for Peter's safety, but they were surprised to see the apostle at the door! Their doubt is understandable. However, it's more fun to ask God for something and then look for things to improve. At the very least, we can believe that God has the power to do anything we ask, and trust him to do what's best.

Ship Ahoy!
Acts 13:1-5

13 AMONG THE PROPHETS and teachers of the church at Antioch were Barnabas and Symeon (also called "The Black Man"), Lucius (from Cyrene), Manaen (the foster-brother of King Herod), and Paul.

2 One day as these men were worshiping and fasting the Holy Spirit said, "Dedicate Barnabas and Paul for a special job I have for them."

3 So after more fasting and prayer, the men laid their hands on them—and sent them on their way.

4 Directed by the Holy Spirit they went to Seleucia and then sailed for Cyprus.

5 There, in the town of Salamis, they went to the Jewish synagogue and preached. (John Mark went with them as their assistant.)

No Tacos, Pizza, or Munchies

To fast means to go without food. (Breakfast actually "breaks a fast"—ends a night without eating.) People sometimes fasted in order to humble themselves before God. They hoped to forget physical needs and concentrate on spiritual matters. A fast might last for one meal, one day or, as with Jesus, forty days.

How Does the Holy Spirit Speak?

Can you read backwards? Try this phrase. If you can't get it, hold it up to a mirror.

ot stnaw tiripS eht yaw ynA
.kaeps

- To one person (Acts 8:29)
- Through other languages (Acts 2:4)
- Through prophets (Acts 11:28)
- Through other disciples (Acts 21:4)
- To a group (Acts 13:2)

The First Missionaries Sail

This is the first time a church selected people and sent them to another place just for the purpose of spreading the Good News of Jesus. The church at Antioch picked two men, Barnabas and Paul. The team asked the young man John Mark and possibly others to assist them. The church may also have sent money to help with the men's expenses.

Sharing Their Pie

It may not have been easy for the leaders at Antioch to give up two of their teachers. There was much to do and the church was growing rapidly (Acts 11:26).

However, the Holy Spirit put their minds on the needs of those far away who had never heard of Jesus. All five seem to have had an attitude of love.

Which Way?

Their first goal was an island named Cyprus. Surrounded by the Mediterranean Sea, it was only 140 miles long by 60 miles wide. It probably took Paul and Barnabas four or five days of sailing to get there.

Homecoming

Barnabas probably loved this trip. The island of Cyprus was his home.

Today a monastery and a church are built on the place where some people believe Barnabas is buried.

Young Person on the Scene

John Mark was related to Barnabas *(Colossians 4:10)*. Barnabas may have been his uncle. Mark originally lived in Jerusalem with his well-to-do mother, Mary. It was his house Peter had gone to when the angel freed him from prison *(Acts 12:12)*.

Mark's life had taken a new turn when Paul and Barnabas brought him to Antioch *(Acts 12:25)*. Now he had a chance for even more travel. Mark was probably excited!

How Can You Help Missionaries Now?

Try not to select more than four of the answers below.

1. Learn more about missions.
2. Give money to missionary work.
3. Chew your cereal loudly so you won't have to think about it.
4. Be a missionary where you are.
5. Pray for missionaries.
6. Save apple cores to mail to missionaries.
7. Name your dog Barnabas.

What Does This Mean to You?

Do You Speak Swahili?

A missionary, according to the dictionary, is a person who is sent to tell a message to people. In one way, Paul and Barnabas were the first missionaries, because they were *sent* to a far land to *tell* about Jesus.

Two thousand years later, churches are still *sending* missionaries to other countries, to preach, teach, translate, farm, do medical work—and *tell* about Jesus. Many missionaries go to language schools so they'll know the language of the people they go to.

Not every missionary signs up to do this for life. One group of doctors figured out a way to be missionaries for short terms. Every year one of the doctors goes to a foreign land to help heal patients and tell them about Jesus Christ. The other three doctors stay home and keep their practice going. The next year another doctor takes his turn and goes overseas.

You can help these missionaries by praying, giving them money, or even writing them letters to encourage them. But you can also be a missionary yourself—and you don't have to learn Swahili. Jesus' command to take his message to one's city and state also applies to you. You've been *sent* with a message to *tell* the people around you. When you talk to them about Jesus and what he means to you, you're just as much of a missionary as those doctors who travel thousands of miles away.

P.S. If you want to say hello in Swahili, say *Jambo*.

Stronger than Sorcery
Acts 13:6-13

6, 7 Afterwards Barnabas and Paul preached from town to town across the entire island until finally they reached Paphos where they met a Jewish sorcerer, a fake prophet named Bar-Jesus. He had attached himself to the governor, Sergius Paulus, a man of considerable insight and understanding. The governor invited Barnabas and Paul to visit him, for he wanted to hear their message from God.

8 But the sorcerer, Elymas (his name in Greek), interfered and urged the governor to pay no attention to what Paul and Barnabas said, trying to keep him from trusting the Lord.

9 Then Paul, filled with the Holy Spirit, glared angrily at the sorcerer and said,

10 "You son of the Devil, full of every sort of trickery and villainy, enemy of all that is good, will you never end your opposition to the Lord?

11 "And now God has laid his hand of punishment upon you, and you will be stricken awhile with blindness." Instantly mist and darkness fell upon him, and he began wandering around begging for someone to take his hand and lead him.

12 When the governor saw what happened he believed and was astonished at the power of God's message.

13 Now Paul and those with him left Paphos by ship for Turkey,[1] landing at the port town of Perga. There John Mark deserted[2] them and returned to Jerusalem.

[1]Literally, "Pamphylia."
[2]Literally, "departed from them." See Acts 15:38.

70

A Willing Ear

The ministry of Barnabas and Paul was attracting so much attention on Cyprus that the news reached the palace. Sergius Paulus, the governor, invited the apostles to come and explain the gospel to him. They were making a big impact on the island.

Funny Name

The prophet had two names: Elymas and Bar-Jesus. Was it wrong for him to have the name of Bar-Jesus?

No. Jesus was a fairly popular name, coming from the Hebrew name, Joshua. Elymas pretended to be a lot of things, but he wasn't pretending to be Jesus.

A Big Mouth

It was bad enough that Bar-Jesus did not want to believe in Jesus. But he didn't want the governor to believe either. Right now the sorcerer had a lot of power over the governor, for the governor believed Bar-Jesus was a prophet.

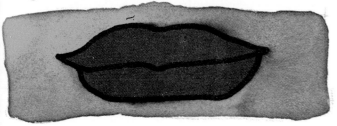

Mixed Feelings

Three men had strong emotions in this passage. Can you match the person and the emotions?

1. urged the governor
2. glared angrily
3. begged for someone   (a) Paul
4. believed   (b) Bar-Jesus
5. attached himself   (c) Sergius Paulus
    to someone
6. astonished at power

Answers: 1. (b) 2. (a) 3. (b) 4. (c) 5. (c) 6. (c)

Is God a Bully?

Was God mean to zap this prophet with blindness? Why didn't he cover Bar-Jesus with flowers, or give him a lifetime supply of chocolate-covered mints? Wouldn't that have changed the mocker's mind?

We can't explain how God thinks, but we do know that some people must be stopped. The man who murders children must be stopped. The kid who steals bicycles must be caught. The person who sells drugs must be arrested.

Not every problem can be solved with gifts of skateboards, apple pie, and two weeks at camp. If people are going to hurt others, they must be stopped.

God decided to act at this time in this way because he wanted to stop Bar-Jesus and allow Sergius Paulus to hear about Jesus Christ.

This blindness wasn't going to last long (verse 11).

Exit John Mark

The way the Bible speaks of Mark's exit from the missionary trip, it doesn't sound like it was planned. Mark suddenly decided to quit, and Paul and Barnabas weren't too happy about it.

Why did he leave after things got exciting at the governor's palace? No one knows. Do you have any ideas?

What Does This Mean to You?

The Battle over You

A church youth group was staying at a hotel in Washington, D.C., one summer weekend. They hoped to be able to go out at night and see the town.

"There is no problem," the hotel manager explained. "If you turn left and stay together, it's perfectly safe. However, don't turn right. That part of town is a little wild."

When they walked outside the choice was tempting. Some wanted to turn right and see what the wild part of town was like. They thought a little danger might be exciting. Fortunately the majority of the group followed the hotel manager's advice.

We often face the same kind of choice in life. Satan stands on one side, calling us, while God stands on the other. Both want us to listen, and sometimes it is a hard decision. Satan seems to have a great deal to offer. But he just wants to use us and destroy us. God wants to help us.

The governor at Paphos heard the voice of Elymas calling him away from Christ. In the end he made the right choice.

A Chance to Play God
Acts 14:8-18

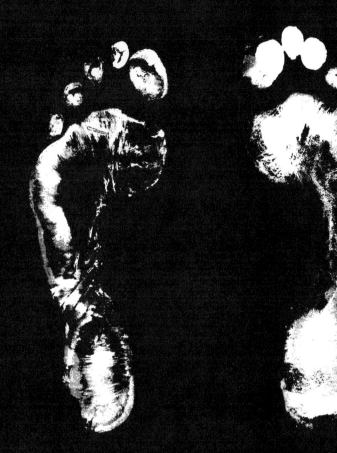

8 While Barnabas and Paul were at Lystra, they came upon a man with crippled feet who had been that way from birth, so he had never walked.

9 He was listening as Paul preached, and Paul noticed him and realized he had faith to be healed!

10 So Paul called to him, "Stand up!" and the man leaped to his feet and started walking!

11 When the listening crowd saw what Paul had done, they shouted (in their local dialect, of course), "These men are gods in human bodies!"

12 They decided that Barnabas was the Greek god Jupiter, and that Paul, because he was the chief speaker, was Mercury!

13 The local priest of the Temple of Jupiter, located on the outskirts of the city, brought them cartloads of flowers and sacrificed oxen to them at the city gates before the crowds.

14 But when Barnabas and Paul saw what was happening they ripped at their clothing in dismay and ran out among the people, shouting,

15 "Men! What are you doing? We are merely human beings like yourselves! We have come to bring you the Good News that you are invited to turn from the worship of these foolish things and to pray instead to the living God who made heaven and earth and sea and everything in them.

16 "In bygone days he permitted the nations to go their own ways,

17 "But he never left himself without a witness; there were always his reminders—the kind things he did such as sending you rain and good crops and giving you food and gladness."

18 But even so, Paul and Barnabas could scarcely restrain the people from sacrificing to them!

Time Slips By

Nearly twenty years have passed since the Book of Acts began. (That may seem like a long time. But travel was very slow.)

Jesus was probably born around 4 B.C., and crucified in A.D. 30.

When Paul and Barnabas arrived in Lystra it was A.D. 49.

An Amazing Advertisement

The apostles had two purposes for healing. One was to show compassion. They really cared for the sick and crippled.

The other reason was to get people's attention, so the apostles could tell about Jesus Christ.

Sky King & Fleet Foot

Myths claimed that the sky god, Jupiter (also known as Zeus), was the chief god. He showed himself to man by thunderbolts. Long ago human beings were sacrificed to him. Barnabas was mistaken for Jupiter.

Mercury's chief job was to be the messenger for the other mythological gods. The crowd called Paul "Mercury" because he seemed to be the chief speaker.

The Flower Necklace

The worshipers of Jupiter felt flowers made a good present for the god. They also usually made a special flower necklace for the sacrificial ox to wear—on its way to dinner.

Rrrrip!

When Jews felt shocked or hurt, they often tore their clothing. They did not tear at their thick outer robes, but ripped the thinner tunics beneath them. News of a death often resulted in tearing.

The tear was usually a small one.

Watermelons on Apple Trees?

One strong reason to believe in a living God is the world around us.

There is order in nature: if you plant an apple tree you do not get watermelons. Nature has design. Leaves and trees are made in particular patterns.

Did the world fall together by accident, or was it made by a Creator?

Paul and Barnabas told their listeners to look around at the rain and the crops and realize that there is a living God.

Nature does not prove there is a God, but it gives us an added reason to believe in him.

Popularity Goes Fast

In Lystra the crowd wanted to worship the apostles. A few days later a mob stoned Paul, dragged him outside of town, and left him for dead (Acts 14:19). All of this happened in the same city. Today a god—tomorrow a criminal.

The Long View

It worked! Despite the confusion, riots, and pain, a group of people in the city of Lystra believed. The apostles appointed elders for this local church (Acts 14:21-23).

Quick Quiz

See how fast and correctly you can answer these short questions:
1. Who was called Mercury?
2. Who was called Jupiter?
3. What did Paul tear?
4. How long had the man been crippled?

Answers: 1. Paul 2. Barnabas 3. Clothing 4. Since birth

What Does This Mean to You?

People on Pedestals

Lisa had a high opinion of the youth director in her church. He had great ideas and was someone you could talk to. But one evening at a party Lisa saw the youth director really lose his temper. He shouted and acted unfairly. Lisa was upset. She considered quitting the youth group.

Once in a while a Christian worker will do something that is very disappointing. He might spread gossip, tell a lie, or forget to keep a promise. It hurts when someone you especially respect lets you down. Yet sooner or later everyone will show his weaker side; he will do something terribly wrong.

All of us are made of the same flimsy material. The best quarterback only completes 60 percent of his passes. The best soprano has trouble hitting the high notes now and then. Barnabas and Paul understood the problem. They wanted everyone to understand from the start that they were just human beings.

You can continue to trust Christian leaders and to respect your friends who know Jesus. But don't put another person on a pedestal, or you'll be crushed when he falls. Only God is worth putting all your hopes on. He'll never let you down.

The Free Gift
Acts 15:1, 2, 4, 6-12, 22, 23

6 So the apostles and chu[rch] elders set a further meeting to decide this question.

7 At the meeting, after lon[g] discussion, Peter stood and addressed them as follows: "Brothers, you all know that G[od] chose me from among you lo[ng] ago to preach the Good News [to] the Gentiles, so that they also could believe.

8 "God, who knows men'[s] hearts, confirmed the fact that [he] accepts Gentiles by giving the[m] the Holy Spirit, just as he gave [it] to us.

9 "He made no distinction between them and us, for he cleansed their lives through fai[th] just as he did ours.

10 "And now are you goi[ng] to correct God by burdening t[he] Gentiles with a yoke that neith[er] we nor our fathers were able [to] bear?

11 "Don't you believe that [all] are saved the same way, by th[e] free gift of the Lord Jesus?"

12 There was no further discussion. . . .

22 Then the apostles and elders and the whole congregation voted to send delegates to Antioch with Paul and Barnabas, to report on thi[s] decision. The men chosen we[re] two of the church leaders—Jud[as] (also called Barsabbas) and Sila[s].

23 They took a letter alon[g] with them: "From: The apostle[s,] elders and brothers at Jerusale[m.] To: The Gentile brothers in Antioch, Syria and Cilicia."

15 WHILE PAUL AND Barnabas were at Antioch, some men from Judea arrived and began to teach the believers that unless they adhered to the ancient Jewish[1] custom of circumcision, they could not be saved.

2 Paul and Barnabas argued and discussed this with them at length, and finally the believers sent them to Jerusalem, accompanied by some local men, to talk to the apostles and elders there about this question. . . .

4 Arriving in Jerusalem, they met with the church leaders—all the apostles and elders were present—and Paul and Barnabas reported on what God had been doing through their ministry. . . .

[1]Literally, "the custom of Moses."

From the Medical Record

Circumcision was the Jewish custom of cutting the foreskin off a male's penis, normally done on the eighth day after birth. God commanded Abraham and all Jewish males to do this as a symbol that the Jews were God's special people *(Genesis 17)*. When Gentile adults were converted to Judaism they were expected to be circumcised.

Today it is a common health practice in the western world to circumcise infant boys. However, Christians have abolished it as a religious practice *(Galatians 5:2)*. Though circumcision set apart the Jews in olden days, the real people of God are now recognized on the basis of faith and God's grace *(Romans 2:28, 29)*.

Choosing Sides

| Men from Judea visited the new Gentile converts at Antioch, and told them they had to become Jews before they could follow Jesus. | Paul and Barnabas said that a Gentile did not have to become a Jew and follow Jewish laws in order to become a Christian. |

Sitting on the Fence

For a while when Peter first was in Antioch, he refused to eat with Gentile Christians because he was afraid of what the stricter Jews would say. Paul scolded Peter for this publicly *(Galatians 2:11)*, and by the time Peter and Paul got back to Jerusalem, Peter was on Paul's side *(Acts 15:10, 11)*.

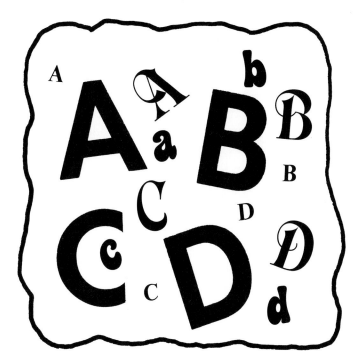

Multiple Choice

1. God showed that he accepted the Gentiles by giving them
   a. credit cards.
   b. the law.
   c. the Holy Spirit.
   d. ten-speed bicycles.
2. Peter compared the Jewish laws to
   a. egg yolks.
   b. a yoke that was too heavy to carry.
   c. an easy obstacle course.
   d. a teacher who gives everyone an A.

Answers: 1. c   2. b

Peter Under Pressure

"Your room's a wreck."

"Can't you ever be on time?"

"That's the loudest noise I've heard since World War II!"

If any of these remarks sound familiar, you know what it's like to be criticized. Someone didn't like what you were doing, and said so.

It's difficult to take criticism. But Peter was able to handle it when Paul said he was wrong. Because of that fact God was able to use Peter to unify the church.

So What?

The decision of the church elders in Acts 15 was what really made Christianity a separate religion from Judaism. If Paul and Barnabas had lost this argument, you might have had to keep all the laws and customs of the Old Testament!

The Jews who believed in Judaism felt that by keeping all the laws, eating all the right things, making sacrifices, and celebrating festivals, they could please God. First of all, that was pretty impossible. Peter called it a yoke they were unable to bear—a burden they couldn't handle.

A second problem was that many Jews kept these laws and customs, but forgot about attitudes of the heart, such as love and compassion and faith, which really please God. Jesus accused the Pharisees of this *(Luke 11:42)*.

Peter explained that what was necessary to please God was to believe in Jesus.

A Circular Letter

The letter from Jerusalem was a circular letter, but that doesn't mean it was written on round paper. A circular letter is one that is meant to be passed around to a number of readers. In this case, many churches throughout Antioch, Syria, and Cilicia read it.

Letters in this time were written on clay tablets, pieces of pottery, or sheets of parchment. Parchment was made from the skins of sheep, goats, and other animals.

This letter didn't have an address or zip code—it was delivered in person.

What Does This Mean to You?

No Brownie Points

You can't earn points with God by being a goody-goody. God doesn't stage tryouts and put the nicest people in the world on his team. He doesn't keep track of everyone's rights and wrongs and then let the people with the least wrongs into heaven.

No one can be good enough to please God because God is perfect. Most of the Jews and Pharisees of Paul's day didn't know that. They tried hard to please God by keeping many laws—and they may have worried that they weren't doing well enough.

If you ever do anything wrong, you're disqualified from any friendship with God—except in one special case.

If you believe that God sent Jesus to die on the cross and pay for all your wrongs, God can accept you—because Jesus promises to give you a whole new life, and to help you serve God.

Does that mean you don't need to be good anymore? No, it doesn't! If you love God because of what he did for you through Jesus, you'll want to live in a way that pleases him. And his laws in the Bible make a good guide for doing just that.

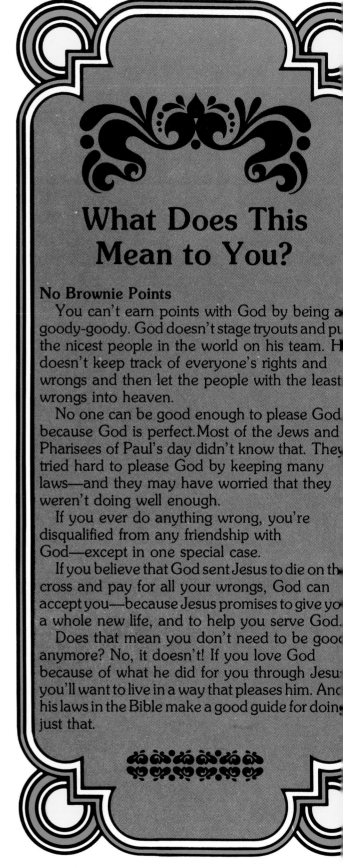

Mission Minus Mark
Acts 15:36-41

36   Several days later Paul suggested to Barnabas that they return again to Turkey, and visit each city where they had preached before,[1] to see how the new converts were getting along.

37   Barnabas agreed, and wanted to take along John Mark.

38   But Paul didn't like that idea at all, since John had deserted them in Pamphylia.

39   Their disagreement over this was so sharp that they separated. Barnabas took Mark with him and sailed for Cyprus,

40,41   While Paul chose Silas and, with the blessing of the believers, left for Syria and Cilicia, to encourage the churches there.

[1]Implied. Literally, "return now and visit every city wherein we proclaimed the word of the Lord."

Mark Jumped Off

This big argument had started in the town of Perga, during the first missionary trip. Mark was traveling with Paul and Barnabas as an assistant, but for some reason decided to leave them.

You Be the Referee

Who was right?

Paul did not want to take anyone on his journey who might quit halfway and hurt the mission.

Barnabas thought Mark deserved a second chance.

If you had had to make this decision, which way would you have chosen?

Double Vision
Double Vision

Despite the argument they had, something good came from this incident. Instead of one missionary group going out, there were now two.
- Team One: Paul and Silas
- Team Two: Barnabas and Mark

Lifeguard on the Lookout

Barnabas's action was no surprise to you if you remembered what Barnabas was like. He enjoyed helping people. One person he had befriended was Paul of Tarsus when others didn't trust the new convert (Acts 9:27).

This is the last time we hear of Barnabas in the Book of Acts.

P.S. A Happy Ending

This may have been a painful experience for Mark, but it worked out happily.

Later we find Mark with Paul when Paul is in prison (Colossians 4:10), and their differences are mended.

Mark also ministered with Timothy (2 Timothy 4:11).

He became a close companion to Peter (1 Peter 5:13). He wrote the Gospel of Mark.

The power of Jesus Christ was at work in Mark's life.

What Does This Mean to You?

Try and Try Again

David Livingstone was one of the most famous missionaries of all time. In the middle 1800s this doctor and explorer dedicated his life to taking the message of Jesus Christ to Africa. But there had been a time when it looked like he would not be a missionary at all.

When Livingstone was training to be a missionary, the instructor wasn't impressed with his pupil's abilities. After three months this man wrote a letter to the mission board, suggesting that the young Scotsman be rejected.

Instead the mission board decided to give Livingstone another chance. If they had not been willing to do that, and if Livingstone had been too discouraged to try again, he might never have sailed for Africa.

Mark may have felt terribly discouraged. After all, he had failed and been rejected by one of the leading Christians in the world. Fortunately he was willing to take a second chance when Barnabas offered it to him.

All of us get rejected. All of us fail sometimes. But that doesn't mean we should give up on ourselves. The real winners are the ones who get up and try again.

The Noisy Slave Girl
Acts 16:16-24

16 One day as we were going with Paul and Silas down to the place of prayer beside the river, we met a demon-possessed slave girl who was a fortune-teller, and earned much money for her masters.

17 She followed along behind us shouting, "These men are servants of God and they have come to tell you how to have your sins forgiven."

18 This went on day after day until Paul, in great distress, turned and spoke to the demon within her. "I command you in the name of Jesus Christ to come out of her," he said. And instantly it left her.

19 Her masters' hopes of wealth were now shattered; they grabbed Paul and Silas and dragged them before the judges at the marketplace.

20, 21 "These Jews are corrupting our city," they shouted. "They are teaching the people to do things that are against the Roman laws."

22 A mob was quickly formed against Paul and Silas, and the judges ordered them stripped and beaten with wooden whips.

23 Again and again the rods slashed down across their bared backs; and afterwards they were thrown into prison. The jailer was threatened with death if they escaped.[1]

24 So he took no chances, but put them into the inner dungeon and clamped their feet into the stocks.

[1]Implied.

Who's "We"?

Luke, the writer of the Book of Acts, is now traveling with Paul and Silas.

Out of Control

Many people in Bible times were controlled by demon spirits. Part of Jesus' ministry was to free people from those terrible influences. Some missionaries today claim to have seen demons possess people. The important fact to remember is that Jesus Christ is more powerful than demons. You don't need to fear them.

Fortune-telling

The slave girl predicted the future for customers. Fortune-telling is still a big business. Many people pay money to have someone look into their palms or into a crystal ball and tell them what will happen tomorrow. People who read horoscopes try the same thing. They want help in understanding the future from someone besides God.

Up the Wall

None of us would have enjoyed what Paul was experiencing. A demon-possessed slave girl followed him around the streets, yelling. Even though what she said was true, she probably scared everyone away from his message.

Paul tried to be patient, but he finally became rattled. The constant shouting was driving him up the wall, and prevented him from getting anything done.

Heartless Crooks

The men who owned this girl did not care about her. When the demons were removed from her, they thought only of their lost money. They became terribly angry when the apostles hurt their purses.

Jesus told us how to best handle our money. He said we should put God first and all the things we need will be added to us *(Matthew 6:33)*. It is easier to be generous toward others when we trust God.

Unpopular Jews

The slave girl's masters were smart to mention Paul's and Silas's nationality to the judges. Feelings at this time were running high against Jews. Emperor Claudius had had all Jews deported from Rome *(Acts 18:2)*.

Being Jewish wasn't in style.

Triple Protection

The prison had three compartments. First came an outer section, fairly open to light and air. The second section was further inside, behind iron gates and bars. Paul and Silas were locked in the third part, a dark dungeon usually reserved for those to be executed. The prisoners' legs were locked in wooden boards with special footholes. A number of holes forced the apostles' feet to be spread far enough apart to cause discomfort and pain.

You're the Editor

One word in each of these sentences needs to be changed. Which word would you correct?
1. She followed along behind them singing.
2. A mob was quickly formed against Paul and Barnabas.
3. Her masters' plans for wealth had now succeeded.
4. "These Jews are decorating our city!"

Answers: Change *decorating* to *corrupting.*
4. Change *succeeded* to *failed.* 3. Change *Barnabas* to *Silas.* 2. Change *singing* to *shouting.* 1. Change

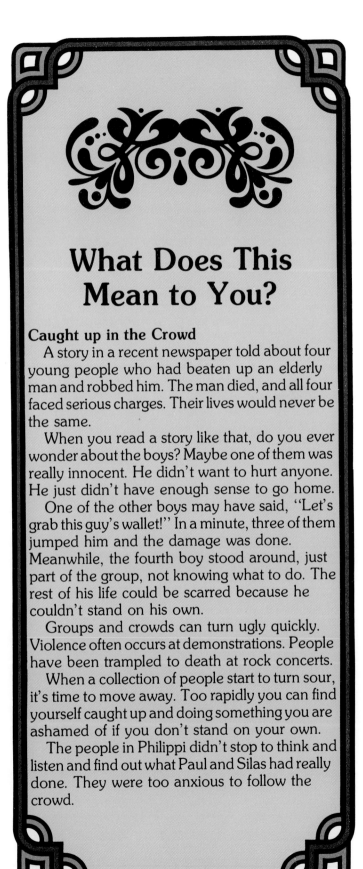

What Does This Mean to You?

Caught up in the Crowd

A story in a recent newspaper told about four young people who had beaten up an elderly man and robbed him. The man died, and all four faced serious charges. Their lives would never be the same.

When you read a story like that, do you ever wonder about the boys? Maybe one of them was really innocent. He didn't want to hurt anyone. He just didn't have enough sense to go home.

One of the other boys may have said, "Let's grab this guy's wallet!" In a minute, three of them jumped him and the damage was done. Meanwhile, the fourth boy stood around, just part of the group, not knowing what to do. The rest of his life could be scarred because he couldn't stand on his own.

Groups and crowds can turn ugly quickly. Violence often occurs at demonstrations. People have been trampled to death at rock concerts.

When a collection of people start to turn sour, it's time to move away. Too rapidly you can find yourself caught up and doing something you are ashamed of if you don't stand on your own.

The people in Philippi didn't stop to think and listen and find out what Paul and Silas had really done. They were too anxious to follow the crowd.

Jailhouse Rock
Acts 16:25-33

25 Around midnight, as Pa[ul] and Silas were praying and singing hymns to the Lord—a[nd] the other prisoners were listening—

26 Suddenly there was a great earthquake; the prison w[as] shaken to its foundations, all th[e] doors flew open—and the chai[ns] of every prisoner fell off!

27 The jailer wakened to se[e] the prison doors wide open, a[nd] assuming the prisoners had escaped, he drew his sword to k[ill] himself.

28 But Paul yelled to him, "Don't do it! We are all here!"

29 Trembling with fear, the jailer called for lights and ran t[o] the dungeon and fell down befor[e] Paul and Silas.

30 He brought them out an[d] begged them, "Sirs, what mus[t I] do to be saved?"

31 They replied, "Believe [on] the Lord Jesus and you will be saved, and your entire household."

32 Then they told him and a[ll] his household the Good News from the Lord.

33 That same hour he washed their stripes and he and a[ll] his family were baptized.

Great Escape Number Three

So far the apostles had made three dramatic escapes from prison, each with miraculous help.

1. An angel had opened the gates for the apostles *(Acts 5:19)*.

2. Peter had needed to be slapped awake when an angel removed his chains *(Acts 12:7)*.

3. An earthquake rocked the entire jail at Philippi, setting Paul and Silas free *(Acts 16:26)*.

#!%$#?&!

Prisoners in those days lived in pain and in miserable conditions. The food and lodging weren't exactly AAA approved. Many prisoners faced possible execution. The bad language the average prisoner used probably could have blistered a bowling ball.

Paul's and Silas's good attitude about prison, as well as their singing, could not have gone unnoticed.

Jailhouse Concert

The apostles were not merely humming softly to themselves. They sang loudly. In the dark dungeon of the jail, prisoners may have enjoyed hearing the duet. Probably no musical group had ever visited this part of town.

On the other hand, some might not have appreciated music in the middle of the night!

What did they sing? The Psalms were high on most Jewish music charts. Paul and Silas had probably memorized them in childhood. As they sang the words, they may have also prayed them.

Everyone Played Statue

The prisoners must have been in shock and unable to run away. They had heard praying and singing, and then felt a rattling earthquake. Standing there totally surprised, they were probably waiting to see what would happen next.

"So Long, World"

It didn't take long for the jailer to sum up the situation. The prison was wide open. He couldn't imagine the prisoners staying. Quickly he drew his sword, intent on killing himself. He knew the Roman government would execute him anyway *(verse 27)*.

Paul yelled out just in time. If he had not said that the prisoners were still there, the jailer would have been a goner.

Word Worm

The jailer asked how he could be saved. He did not need to be saved from punishment by Roman law, because the prisoners had not escaped.

What did "saved" mean?

If we save stamps or save autographs, we collect them and put them away for safekeeping. We make sure they are not lost, damaged, or destroyed.

When Jesus saves us he does the same thing. He protects people from being lost forever. We are saved by asking Jesus to forgive our sins and give us the new life that never ends *(Acts 16:31; Romans 5:8, 9)*.

Joke Time

Q. How were the jail doors like birds?

A. ·(uǝdo) ʍǝlɟ ʎǝɥʇ

Ring around the Collar

Jails were miserable, dirty places. The apostles had not washed, so dried blood was probably still caked on their backs from their beatings. The jailer helped out by washing it off.

What Does This Mean to You?

Songs in the Night

Cleaning the house wasn't one of Wendy's favorite jobs, but you would never have guessed it to hear her. Hair wrapped in a scarf, she whisked the dustrag across the furniture and hummed to herself.

Wendy had a way of turning a miserable situation into an adventure. The key was her attitude.

Not every day can be surfing along the shore. Not every meal is hamburgers and fries. Not every trip to the store is for designer jeans. Some days are simply bummers. We have to struggle through some things whether we like them or not.

That's when a sampling of songs or hymns comes in handy. A happy attitude helps pass the time much better than a frown or a sharp tongue.

How do you even get into the mood to sing? On a day when King David was feeling down, he wrote, "By day the Lord directs his love, at night his song is with me" *(Psalm 42:8, New International Version)*. God can help you have a song in the night if you ask him.

The Mystery God
cts 17:16, 19, 22, 23, 29-32

16 Some time later, while Paul was in Athens, he was deeply troubled by all the idols he saw everywhere throughout the city. . . .

19 The people invited him to the forum at Mars Hill. "Come and tell us more about this new religion," they said. . . .

22 So Paul addressed them as follows: "Men of Athens, I notice that you are very religious,

23 "For as I was out walking I saw your many altars, and one of them had this inscription on it—'To the Unknown God.' You have been worshiping him without knowing who he is, and now I wish to tell you about him. . . .

29 "We shouldn't think of God as an idol made by men from gold or silver or chipped from stone.

30 "God tolerated man's past ignorance about these things, but now he commands everyone to put away idols and worship only him.

31 "For he has set a day for justly judging the world by the man he has appointed, and has pointed him out by bringing him back to life again."

32 When they heard Paul speak of the resurrection of a person who had been dead, some laughed, but others said, "We want to hear more about this later."

Brain City

Athens was a fantastic city for thinkers. Four and five hundred years before Christ some of the great minds of all time lived there. Socrates, Plato, Aristotle, Epicurus, and Zeno are just a few.

When Paul arrived there the Athenians still considered themselves among the best minds.

Idea Taster

The people of Athens liked to sample ideas just as we like to pick from salad bars. If someone had a new or interesting idea to present, they loved to hear it. They were curious and probably amused by Paul's presentation.

Mars Hill

This hill was named after the Greek war god, Mars.

Stamp of Approval

The forum which met on Mars Hill could not have arrested Paul. However, their opinion was very valuable. If a speaker's thinking was laughed at by this group, many others would find it hard to accept.

Idle Idols

Idols come in different sizes and forms. Some are beautifully made, and others are hideous and monstrous.

An idol is an object which people believe has supernatural powers. They might even believe their god lives in the idol. Carved idols were common in Paul's time.

Short Sermon?

The Bible shows a small version of Paul's sermon. It was probably much longer.

Tele-code

You can fill in the blank in the sentence below by using your telephone dial to break the code. Each number stands for a letter near it on the phone dial. But be careful: you must correctly guess which of the dial letters is the right one to use!

The men of _ _ _ _ _ _ were very religious.

2 8 4 3 6 7

Answer : Athens

The "What If" God

What if the people at Athens were wrong? What if, in all their talk of religion and philosophy, they missed the real God?

No problem, as they saw it. They merely built an extra monument to "the unknown god," just in case. They didn't want to take any chances.

Mixed Reviews

Some who heard Paul said his words were nonsense. Others said they would like to hear more later. Another group later believed in Jesus Christ.

What Does This Mean to You?

Building Bridges

Sometimes we would like to talk about our faith with a friend, but we don't know where to start. One way is to do what Paul did at Mars Hill. He began where his audience was. They believed in an "unknown god," so Paul discussed him and then led the conversation to Jesus Christ.

You may be talking with a friend about someone who cheated on a test. You could ask your friend how he or she decides what's right and wrong—and then lead the conversation to your belief in a God who makes standards to help us.

You might be listening to a friend worry, and ask for his or her opinion on who controls the future. Then you could tell about God's hand on your future, and the peace that gives you.

This is called bridge building. We construct a road from where the person is and what he already understands, and lead to what he needs to know about God and Jesus.

Nasty Words
cts 18:1-8

THEN PAUL LEFT Athens and
nt to Corinth.

2, 3 There he became
quainted with a Jew named
quila, born in Pontus, who had
cently arrived from Italy with his
fe, Priscilla. They had been
pelled from Italy as a result of
audius Caesar's order to deport
Jews from Rome. Paul lived
d worked with them, for they
re tentmakers just as he was.

4 Each Sabbath found Paul at
e synagogue, trying to convince
e Jews and Greeks alike.

5 And after the arrival of Silas
d Timothy from Macedonia,
ul spent his full time preaching
d testifying to the Jews that
sus is the Messiah.

6 But when the Jews
posed him and blasphemed,
rling abuse at Jesus, Paul shook
f the dust from his robe and said,
our blood be upon your own
ads—I am innocent—from
w on I will preach to the
entiles."

7 After that he stayed with
tus Justus, a Gentile[1] who
orshiped God and lived next
oor to the synagogue.

8 Crispus, the leader of the
nagogue, and all his household
lieved in the Lord and were
ptized—as were many others in
orinth.

plied.

Tough Tentmaking

- The tents Paul made were probably sewn from goat-hair cloth.
- As with most young men, Paul probably learned his trade from his parents.
- The job consisted of sewing lengths of cloth together and adding ropes and loops.
- Paul probably had tough, calloused hands.

Empty Wallets?

It was difficult for the apostles to make a living. Sometimes they could stay with other believers. But often they were beaten, jailed, and run out of town.

Many times Paul made tents to earn money. At other times he accepted gifts from churches to keep him going *(2 Corinthians 11:7-9)*.

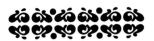

Which Is Which?

Priscilla is the woman's name. She is often called Prisca.

Aquila is the man's name. It is also the Roman word meaning eagle.

Persecution of the Jews

Emperor Claudius ordered that all Jews must leave Rome in A.D. 49 or 50. Long disliked, the Jews were involved in riots among themselves just before they were expelled. Aquila and Priscilla were among those forced to leave. There may have been twenty thousand Jews in Rome at the time.

Pearls and Pigs

People began to abuse the name of Jesus early. Unwilling to believe in him, they decided to say crude, ugly things about the Lord.

When people are nasty and insulting about Jesus Christ, it might be best to walk away, as Paul did. If someone refuses to listen to God's Good News, we could be wasting our time while they make fun of us.

This seems to be the meaning of what Jesus said when he told us not to cast pearls before swine (*Matthew 7:6*). If we wait until another day, such a person might be more willing to hear us.

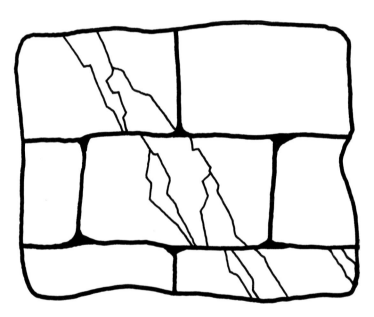

The Wall Cracked

People at the synagogue opposed the Gospel of Jesus Christ, and were even crude about Jesus' name. However, their wall of resistance soon began to crack.

Crack one: Titus Justus, who lived next door to the synagogue, became a Christian.

Crack two: Crispus, the ruler of the synagogue, believed. Paul then baptized him (*1 Corinthians 1:14*).

The flood: Many others believed.

Where?

1. Aquila and Priscilla moved away from what country?
2. Crispus lived in what city?
3. Titus Justus lived next door to what?

Answers: 1. Italy 2. Corinth 3. the synagogue

What Does This Mean to You?

God's Undercover Work

What is the worst thing you have ever been called because you are a Christian? Has anyone ever become really upset with you because of what you believe? Did you feel like giving up on talking to that person?

Don't be surprised if someone throws a few strong words at you. Nonbelievers did it to Jesus, Paul, and many other Christians.

Words can really hurt, but they usually pass over like a storm, and you go on living. Words shouldn't stop you from acting like a Christian toward a person, even if you can't talk to him or her about Jesus.

Interestingly, the kid who calls you or your God names today might become a Christian tomorrow. Sometimes God is working inside people when you'd never guess it from the outside, just as he was in Corinth.

Later the same person who acted nasty to you may soften his attitude and want to hear about Christ. A gentle, patient spirit on your part can make it easier for him to do that.

Black Magic Bonfire
Acts 19:1, 13-20

19 Paul traveled through Turkey and arrived in Ephesus.
. . .

13 A team of itinerant Jews who were traveling from town to town casting out demons planned to experiment by using the name of the Lord Jesus. The incantation they decided on was this: "I adjure you by Jesus, whom Paul preaches, to come out!"

14 Seven sons of Sceva, a Jewish priest, were doing this.

15 But when they tried it on a man possessed by a demon, the demon replied, "I know Jesus and I know Paul, but who are you?"

16 And he leaped on two of them and beat them up, so that they fled out of his house naked and badly injured.

17 The story of what happened spread quickly all through Ephesus, to Jews and Greeks alike; and a solemn fear descended on the city, and the name of the Lord Jesus was greatly honored.

18, 19 Many of the believers who had been practicing black magic confessed their deeds and brought their incantation books and charms and burned them at a public bonfire. (Someone estimated the value of the books at $10,000.)

20 This indicates how deeply the whole area was stirred by God's message.

Don't Sneeze!

Groups of performers often strolled around the countryside offering cures and telling fortunes—for a price, as the sons of Sceva did.

One first-century magician named Eleazar is supposed to have drawn a demon out of a person's nose. He then had the demon knock over a glass of water to prove he was real.

The Exorcists

These men claimed to have the power to merely say a phrase and cause a demon to come out of a person. Some people still claim this power today. Movies about demons and exorcists are popular.

The apostles had power from God over demons, and used it. Paul chased a demon out of a slave girl *(Acts 16:18)*.

For the Fun of It

Itinerant means to travel from place to place. How many words can you get out of *itinerant* without changing the order of the letters?

ITINERANT

Stay on Guard

Not everyone who uses the name of Jesus is really a Christian.

Jesus knew that men would attempt to heal and cast out demons in his name. Some would be phonies who were just using the words, while others were true believers *(Matthew 7:22)*.

The name of Jesus and the words of the Bible carry a lot of weight. Many cult leaders use certain parts of the Bible or quote a few words of Jesus just to make their own group sound good.

A Real Hair-Raiser

Word raced around town; someone had used the name of Jesus, and it had backfired on him. When people mentioned Jesus later, their tone of voice was probably more respectful.

Everything You Want to Know about . . .

Some of the books the Ephesians burned may have dealt with these secret formulas:

- splanchnomancy—how to study animal entrails in order to predict the future
- necromancy—how to talk to the spirits of the dead
- belomancy—how to throw arrows on the ground to read the future
- rabdomancy—how to let two sticks fall to the ground and know their meaning
- astrology—how to study the stars to predict the future
- idolmancy—how to hear idols speak

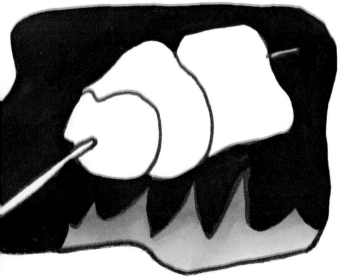

Roasted Marshmallows, Anyone?

The large cost of the materials suggests that many magic books were burned in this huge bonfire.

Today thousands of people still spend money on magic or fortune-telling books. Most major newspapers carry horoscope columns, and billions of dollars are spent on astrology books.

If a large city had this type of bonfire today they could probably save a lot of money on heating bills.

What Does This Mean to You?

A Lot of Hogwash

If you are a superstitious person, you can easily become a nervous wreck. Before you leave the house in the morning, you have to check your horoscope to make sure the stars are right for what you're planning, and to learn what kind of day you're going to have. Unless it's Friday the thirteenth; in that case, you'll probably stay at home.

You have to make sure a rabbit's foot is in your purse or pocket. Don't slam the door, or you might break a mirror and bring on bad luck for years. If it's raining, don't open your umbrella in the house—that could bring death.

Once outside, walk carefully, avoiding ladders and black cats. . . .

"Why would anyone practice that sort of thing?" you may ask. "It seems like a lot of hogwash."

People get involved in the occult and in superstition because they want to have some knowledge of, or control over, the future. But as you can see, superstition soon begins controlling them.

One benefit of belonging to Jesus Christ is that we don't need to worry about our tomorrows. Each of us is safe in the Son of God. One popular saying is worth remembering: "I don't know what the future holds, but I know who holds the future."

Not Good for Business
Acts 19:23-31

23 About that time, a big blowup developed in Ephesus concerning the Christians.

24 It began with Demetrius, a silversmith who employed many craftsmen to manufacture silver shrines of the Greek goddess Diana.

25 He called a meeting of his men, together with others employed in related trades, and addressed them as follows: "Gentlemen, this business is our income.

26 "As you know so well from what you've seen and heard, this man Paul has persuaded many, many people that handmade gods aren't gods at all. As a result, our sales volume is going down! And this trend is evident not only here in Ephesus, but throughout the entire province!

27 "Of course, I am not only talking about the business aspects of this situation and our loss of income, but also of the possibility that the temple of the great goddess Diana will lose its influence, and that Diana—this magnificent goddess worshiped not only throughout this part of Turkey but all around the world—will be forgotten!"

28 At this their anger boile and they began shouting, "Gre is Diana of the Ephesians!"

29 A crowd began to gath and soon the city was filled wi confusion. Everyone rushed to the amphitheater, dragging alo Gaius and Aristarchus, Paul's traveling companions, for trial.

30 Paul wanted to go in, b the disciples wouldn't let him.

31 Some of the Roman officers of the province, friends Paul, also sent a message to hi begging him not to risk his life entering.

A Wonder of the World

The temple to Diana in Ephesus was so magnificent, it was considered one of the seven wonders of the world. It was a beautiful building surrounded by one hundred columns. Its ruined site can still be seen in Ephesus today.

Six More Wonders

The other six wonders of the ancient world were:

1. *The pyramids of Egypt.*
2. *The hanging gardens of Babylon.* This forest on a 75-foot wall had to be irrigated by water pumped up by slaves. King Nebuchadnezzar built it for a mountain princess he married, to make her less homesick.
3. *The statue of Zeus at Olympia, Greece.* Zeus, sitting on his throne, measured 40 feet high and was made of ivory and gold.
4. *The tomb of Mausolus in Turkey.* This huge marble structure is what all mausoleums are named after.
5. *The Colossus of Rhodes.* This 120-foot bronze statue of the sun god guarded the harbor of Rhodes. It would have been about the size of the Statue of Liberty.
6. *The lighthouse of Alexandria, Egypt.* This structure was 440 feet high, and had a fire burning on top to give light to ships.

Of the seven wonders of the ancient world, only the pyramids of Egypt remain standing today.

Moon Princess

Her Latin name was Diana. Often she is discussed under her Greek name, Artemis. In Greek and Roman mythology, Diana was the moon goddess, and was supposed to be in charge of women's lives, childbearing, young animals, and hunting, among other things.

Paperweights

These temple images were probably like the metal copies you might own of the White House, Capitol Building, or Washington Monument. They were souvenirs: silver replicas of the Shrine of Diana. The miniatures may have been dedicated in the temple. Some images of the shrine have been found in the ruins of Ephesus, but so far no silver ones. The silver ones were probably melted down many centuries ago.

What Is an Idol?

Meaning one: Any man-made object which people worship as a god.

Meaning two: Anything which becomes more important to us than God.

Stone from Outer Space

A gigantic stone was placed over the entrance of the temple of Diana. Some people believed it was sent down from the sky by Diana herself.

We cannot be certain, but this stone may have been a meteorite. If so, this would not be the first religion to use a meteorite as part of worship.

Worship Was Gross

Diana was worshiped in many places in the Middle East and Europe over a long time. The ideas about what she did and how to please her varied. Here are a few of the ways she was honored:

- In very early times, people were sacrificed to her.
- The Spartans offered her goats before battle.
- Before marriage young girls would offer Diana a lock of hair, a belt, and a dress.

Shrinking Money

Teaching the love of God often changed the economy. Jesus chased money changers out of the temple *(Matthew 21:12)*. When Paul removed the demon from the slave girl, he hurt her masters' income *(Acts 16:19)*. Now the silver idolatry business at Ephesus was about to shrink.

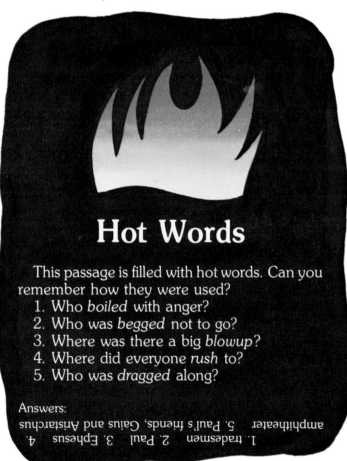

Hot Words

This passage is filled with hot words. Can you remember how they were used?

1. Who *boiled* with anger?
2. Who was *begged* not to go?
3. Where was there a big *blowup*?
4. Where did everyone *rush* to?
5. Who was *dragged* along?

Answers:

1. tradesmen 2. Paul 3. Ephesus 4. amphitheater 5. Paul's friends, Gaius and Aristarchus

What Does This Mean to You?

Dollar Signs in Their Eyes

It isn't difficult to figure out why some people hand out drugs to kids. They want the kids to try them. If a kid likes drugs and gets hooked on them, he becomes a new market. A market means money for the pusher.

Pushers call kids cowards if the kids don't want the drugs. Pushers talk about growing up, and about freedom. That is what they say, but it's a cover-up. Their major interest is money.

It must hurt when a drug pusher sees someone become a Christian. The pusher knows he has probably just lost a customer.

Beware of people with dollar signs in their eyes, who only care about you for what they can get from you. Beware that you don't grow dollar signs in your own eyes and stop caring about others!

Snoring in Church
Acts 20:1, 6-12

20 WHEN IT WAS all over, Paul sent for the disciples, preached a farewell message to them, said good-bye and left for Greece. . . .

6 As soon as the Passover ceremonies ended, we boarded ship at Philippi in northern Greece and five days later arrived in Troas, Turkey, where we stayed a week.

7 On Sunday, we gathered for a Communion service, with Paul preaching. And since he was leaving the next day, he talked until midnight!

8 The upstairs room where we met was lighted with many flickering lamps;

9 And as Paul spoke on and on, a young man named Eutychus, sitting on the window sill, went fast asleep and fell three stories to his death below.

10, 11, 12 Paul went down and took him into his arms. "Don't worry," he said, "he's all right!" And he was! What a wave of awesome joy swept through the crowd! They all went back upstairs and ate the Lord's Supper together; then Paul preached another long sermon— so it was dawn when he finally left them!

Snore for Sure

The conditions were perfect to put Eutychus to sleep.
- The room was warm.
- It was crowded.
- The smell of lamps was heavy.
- It was past midnight.
- The sermon was long.

All totaled, it was almost a guaranteed trip to slumberville.

Open Windows

Windows in those days did not have glass. Instead, they were often covered by wooden shutters called lattices. These swung open easily.

A Double Meal

The Communion gathering they celebrated may have had two parts. Often Christians ate a meal together and then passed the bread and wine for Communion.

Eating was frequently a part of a Christian gathering and fellowship.

A Rebus Quiz

Where was the sermon delivered?

Answer: a three-story house

Shifting to Sunday

This service is evidence for the beginning of a change from traditional Jewish Saturday worship to Sundays, in honor of Jesus' resurrection day. The apostle John later writes of "the Lord's day" *(Revelation 1:10).*

Tongue Torture

It's hard to find anyone named Eutychus today. However, if you do decide to name your son this, pronounce it *YOU-tick-us.*

Dozing Off

Anyone who has fallen asleep in public knows this is a slow, agonizing situation. Your eyelids begin to get heavy. The speaker's or teacher's words become lost in a drone. Everything feels warm, and suddenly, you're out.

When you wake up you feel embarrassed. You hope that no one noticed—and that you didn't snore.

A Young Man

Eutychus may have been close to your age. The Greek word used here normally describes someone eight to fourteen years old.

What Does This Mean to You?

Stay-awake Tips

Probably not many of you have fallen out of a church balcony or snored during the pastor's sermon. But you know it can sometimes be a fight to stay awake in church.

What can you do to stay awake on a drowsy morning? Paper airplanes are not the solution. Bringing a pet lizard seems out of place. However, there are a few steps you can take that might give you some pep:

Skip the midnight movie. It's hard for anyone to stay awake anywhere when he didn't go to bed until 2:00 A.M. the night before.

Bring a pad and paper. If you keep notes, you become involved in the sermon instead of sitting back like a stone block.

Ask what the service means to you. Instead of looking around, look at yourself. The sermon might have just the help you were looking for, or it might answer questions you've asked.

These are just a few suggestions. Maybe you can think of more.

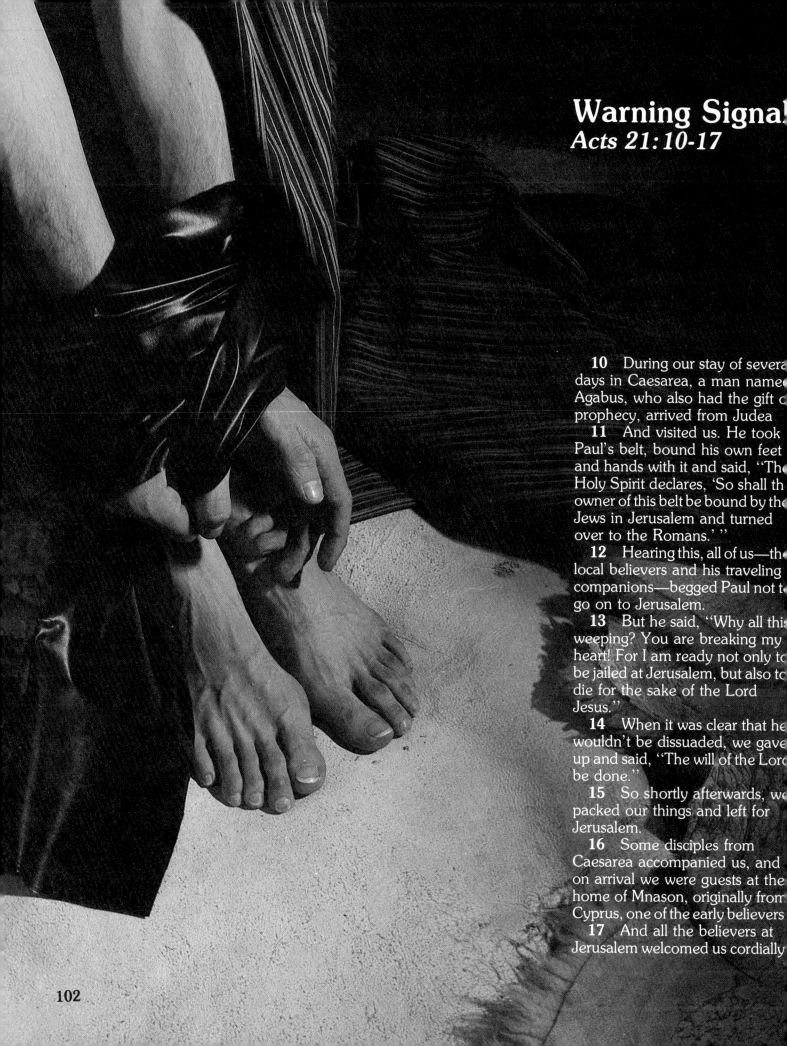

Warning Signal
Acts 21:10-17

10 During our stay of several days in Caesarea, a man named Agabus, who also had the gift of prophecy, arrived from Judea

11 And visited us. He took Paul's belt, bound his own feet and hands with it and said, "The Holy Spirit declares, 'So shall the owner of this belt be bound by the Jews in Jerusalem and turned over to the Romans.'"

12 Hearing this, all of us—the local believers and his traveling companions—begged Paul not to go on to Jerusalem.

13 But he said, "Why all this weeping? You are breaking my heart! For I am ready not only to be jailed at Jerusalem, but also to die for the sake of the Lord Jesus."

14 When it was clear that he wouldn't be dissuaded, we gave up and said, "The will of the Lord be done."

15 So shortly afterwards, we packed our things and left for Jerusalem.

16 Some disciples from Caesarea accompanied us, and on arrival we were guests at the home of Mnason, originally from Cyprus, one of the early believers

17 And all the believers at Jerusalem welcomed us cordially

Hit the Nail on the Head

Paul's friends knew that Agabus wasn't just guessing about the future. He was a prophet. Years before, he had predicted that a great famine would hit Israel *(Acts 11:28)*. And the famine had come exactly as Agabus said it would.

A Funny-looking

Paul's belt was a piece of clothing that served many purposes. It was a wide piece of cloth or leather tied around the waist to hold loose-fitting clothes together. Money was often tucked into it for safekeeping. If a man carried a weapon, it also fit snugly in his belt.

Peculiar Prophets

Agabus wasn't the first prophet to do something physical to make a point. Isaiah walked naked and barefoot around Egypt, at God's orders, to tell the Egyptians they would be captured by Assyria *(Isaiah 20:2)*. He did that for a chilly three years!

The prophet Ahijah tore his new robe into twelve pieces to show that the tribes of Israel would be taken out of Solomon's hands and split up *(I Kings 11:29-31)*.

Ezekiel shaved his head and beard to show that God planned to punish Israel's wickedness publicly *(Ezekiel 5:1-7)*.

Opinion Poll

Do you think Paul was foolish? No one seemed to believe he should go to Jerusalem. His Christian friends tried to talk him out of it.

And Paul's trip to Jerusalem did cause a terrible uproar and a tremendous riot. All the trouble Agabus predicted came true, including his arrest.

Do you think Paul could have done more good if he had stayed away?

What Does This Mean to You?

God's Voice

Have you ever heard God speak to you? Has he ever told you to go to Toledo, or asked you to straighten your room? Has God said it out loud so that you could hear him?

Paul felt the Holy Spirit urging him to go to Jerusalem *(Acts 20:22)*, and wanted to obey in spite of his friends' advice. The Bible has many examples of God speaking to people with his voice, but there are other ways for God to speak.

There was a girl who volunteered to teach a class because she started to care about the students. She felt God put the "care" inside her, and that was his way of speaking.

A boy walked toward an enemy of his and offered to be his friend. In a few minutes they were playing basketball together. The boy had read the Bible, and it told him to love his enemies. He felt the Bible was God's way of speaking to him.

Sometimes God can speak to us in the advice of parents and Christian friends.

We probably will never hear a voice talking to us from heaven. But that doesn't mean God isn't saying anything.

26, 27 Paul on the next day went with the men to the temple for the ceremony, thus publicizing his vow to offer a sacrifice seven[1] days later with the others. The seven days were almost ended when some Jews from Turkey saw him in the temple and roused a mob against him. They grabbed him,

28 Yelling, "Men of Israel! Help! Help! This is the man who preaches against our people and tells everybody to disobey the Jewish laws. He even talks against the temple and defiles it by bringing Gentiles in!"

29 (For down in the city earlier that day, they had seen him with Trophimus, a Gentile[2] from Ephesus in Turkey, and assumed that Paul had taken him into the temple.)

30 The whole population of the city was electrified by these accusations and a great riot followed. Paul was dragged out of the temple, and immediately the gates were closed behind him.

31 As they were killing him, word reached the commander of the Roman garrison that all Jerusalem was in an uproar.

32 He quickly ordered out his soldiers and officers and ran down among the crowd. When the mob saw the troops coming, they quit beating Paul.

33 The commander arrested him and ordered him bound with double chains. Then he asked the crowd who he was and what he had done.

34 Some shouted one thing and some another. When he couldn't find out anything in all the uproar and confusion, he ordered Paul to be taken to the armory.[3]

35 As they reached the stairs the mob grew so violent that the soldiers lifted Paul to their shoulders to protect him,

36 And the crowd surged behind shouting, "Away with him, away with him!"

[1] Literally, "the days of purification."
[2] Implied.
[3] Literally, "castle," or "fort."

Paul Goes Bald

To prove he wasn't anti-Jewish, Paul agreed to take a Nazirite vow with four other men *(Acts 21:23)*.

As part of the vow, Paul
- shaved his head bald
- drank no wine
- made animal sacrifices
- was not supposed to cut his hair again during the vow.

A Nazirite vow was a ritual of dedication to God, asking God for spiritual strength. Such vows often lasted 30 days, but could be much longer. The Old Testament muscle man, Samson, was a Nazirite all his life until he broke the vow by letting Delilah cut his hair *(Judges 16:16, 17)*.

Gentiles Beware

If Paul had taken a Gentile into the temple he would have broken the Jewish law, and defiled the temple. The two could go into the Court of Gentiles, but the area beyond that was forbidden. Written notices informed a Gentile that he could be executed for entering.

The Rumor Express

Few things can travel as fast as a rumor. The whole population was buzzing about Paul's dastardly deed, and they nearly killed him.

The worst part was that the story wasn't true.

Romans to the Rescue

A Roman garrison was stationed nearby. Normally such a garrison had 200 soldiers in it.

When the soldiers came to settle the big uproar in Jerusalem, the crowd was killing Paul. It was one time the apostle was thrilled to be arrested!

Word Worm

Calvary is the name of the hill where Jesus was crucified.

Cavalry means a troop of soldiers on horseback.

Each word has exactly the same letters.

What Does This Mean to You?

Watch out for the Birdie

One of the ugliest birds in the world is the Flying Rumor. An energetic creature, it manages to get around more quickly than a speeding bullet.

As the foulest of the fowl, the Flying Rumor has been known to tear at reputations, pull friendships apart, and generally smear personalities. The Flying Rumor may coo like a dove, but it stinks like a vulture. It is never to be trusted. Its smile is only a disguise for a cruel beak.

The Flying Rumor was nearly successful at destroying Paul. It has been known to wreck others.

If you sight this gruesome bird, do not feed it. Don't even allow it to land. Don't pass it on. Just shoot it down.

Murder Plot
Acts 22:30; 23:9-18, 23, 24

30 The next day the commander freed Paul from hi chains and ordered the chief priests into session with the Jewi Council. He had Paul brought before them to try to find out wh the trouble was all about. . . .

9 There a great clamor aros . . .

10 The shouting grew loud and louder, and the men were tugging at Paul from both side Finally the commander, fearing they would tear him apart, ordered his soldiers to take hir away from them by force and bring him back to the armory.

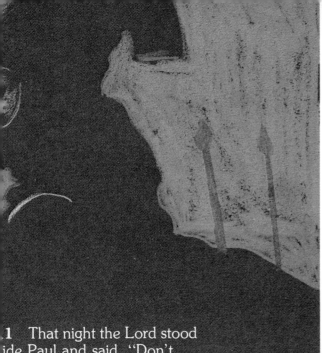

1 That night the Lord stood [bes]ide Paul and said, "Don't [wor]ry, Paul; just as you have told [the] people about me here in [Jer]usalem, so you must also in [Ro]me."

[1]2, 13 The next morning [som]e 40 or more of the Jews got [tog]ether and bound themselves [with] a curse neither to eat nor drink [unt]il they had killed Paul!

[1]4 Then they went to the [chi]ef priests and elders and told [the]m what they had done.

[1]5 "Ask the commander to [brin]g Paul back to the Council [aga]in," they requested. "Pretend [yo]u want to ask a few more [que]stions. We will kill him on the [wa]y."

[1]6 But Paul's nephew got [win]d of their plan and came to the [arm]ory and told Paul.

[1]7 Paul called one of the [offi]cers and said, "Take this boy [to t]he commander. He has [som]ething important to tell him."

[1]8 So the officer did, . . .

[2]3, 24 Then the commander [cal]led two of his officers and [ord]ered, "Get 200 soldiers ready [to l]eave for Caesarea at nine [o'c]lock tonight! Take 200 [spe]armen and 70 mounted [cav]alry. Give Paul a horse to ride [an]d get him safely to Governor [Fel]ix."

Brain Strain

Question: How did Paul's nephew get in to see the apostle?

Answer: Often visitors were allowed to take food, clothing, and books to prisoners.

A Huge Bodyguard

How many men did it take to escort Paul out of range of the people who wanted to murder him?

Spearmen	200
Horsemen	70
Total	270 men

The Romans had a great respect for large, angry crowds. That night 200 men headed back to Jerusalem. The 70 horsemen continued to guard Paul, from Antipatris to Caesarea.

Paul's Close Calls

The apostle is nearly killed several times in Acts 21 through 23.

- Agabus predicted hard times at Jerusalem *(Acts 21:10, 11)*.
- Paul was almost beaten to death outside the temple *(Acts 21:31)*.
- The Romans started to whip Paul *(Acts 22:25)*.
- The Council tried to tear Paul apart *(Acts 23:10)*.
- More than forty men swore to not eat until they killed Paul *(Acts 23:12, 13)*.

Two Heroes

Without the help of Roman soldiers, Paul almost certainly would have been killed by the Jews. The commander who came to the rescue by first arresting Paul was Claudius Lysias. He had paid to become a Roman citizen.

And without Paul's nephew's sharp ears and courage, the commander would not have known to whisk Paul out of town for his safety.

A Tough Diet

At least forty men vowed not to eat a crumb or drink a drop until Paul was dead. But the apostle probably lived for ten years after this incident.

If they had stayed on their "diet," these men would soon have been skinny people.

The Midnight Ride of Paul

The apostle rode on a horse from Jerusalem to Caesarea. It was a sixty-mile trip.

What Does This Mean to You?

Heroes

How much difference can one person make in the world? Many of us feel like a small number in a huge computer, like a drop of ink in the ocean. But it is amazing how much effect one person can have. Anyone can be a hero.

Frank Laubach was one small individual who tried to use the abilities God gave him. He devised a new system to teach people how to read. And during his lifetime alone, sixty million people learned to read through this system. All over the world people were introduced to the Bible because of Laubach's reading approach.

The Bible only mentions Paul's nephew once. Yet he was a hero. When he saved the apostle's life, he allowed many more people to hear about Jesus Christ than would have if Paul had been killed.

Each of us is important in God's eyes, and can do something for him. One person can help erase prejudice in his school. One person can simply refuse to pass on a rumor or a lie. One person can be a friend to a lonely newcomer. One person can back off when others are planning vandalism.

God is eager to use each of us. We can all be heroes when we serve him. Sometimes even the small things we do turn out to be more important than we think.

oolish Felix
cts 24:22-27

22 Felix, who knew Christians didn't go around starting riots,[1] told the Jews to wait for the arrival of Lysias, the garrison commander, and then he would decide the case.

23 He ordered Paul to prison but instructed the guards to treat him gently and not to forbid any of his friends from visiting him or bringing him gifts to make his stay more comfortable.

24 A few days later Felix came with Drusilla, his legal[2] wife, a Jewess. Sending for Paul, they listened as he told them about faith in Christ Jesus.

25 And as he reasoned with them about righteousness and self-control and the judgment to come, Felix was terrified. "Go away for now," he replied, "and when I have a more convenient time, I'll call for you again."

26 He also hoped that Paul would bribe him, so he sent for him from time to time and talked with him.

27 Two years went by in this way; then Felix was succeeded by Porcius Festus. And because Felix wanted to gain favor with the Jews, he left Paul in chains.

[1]Literally, "having more accurate knowledge."
[2]Literally, "his own wife."

Government Scandal

Felix's wife Drusilla had originally been married to the king of Emesa. But at age 16 she left her husband to marry Felix.

Drusilla probably hadn't learned much about right and wrong while growing up. Her father was Herod Agrippa I, a member of the bloodthirsty Herod family.

This was at least a second marriage for Drusilla and the third wife for Felix.

What Do You Think?

Was Paul frustrated to be in prison instead of on his way to Rome? He was stuck in one place because of selfish Felix.

How would you have felt in Paul's place?

Knowing Paul, how do you think he spent his time in jail?

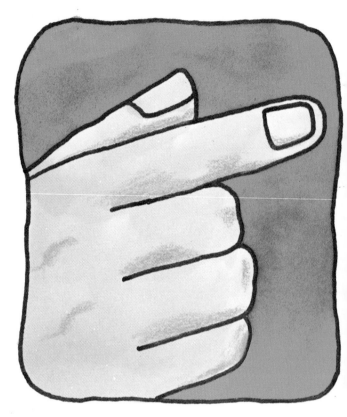

Paul Pointed a Finger

The apostle probably did not give Felix a long message explaining Christianity. Judging by Felix's reaction, Paul's words were pointed, and concerned the type of sin Felix and Drusilla had committed.

When Paul finished, Felix was shaking in his sandals.

Felix Plays Dodge

Paul's subject got too hot for the governor. Felix decided to dodge the question of becoming a Christian. He told Paul he would hear more from him when he wasn't so busy.

Bribes Are Bad

bribe is a price paid to et something done which should not be done.

Bribes are bad because they encourage greed and unfair favors.

he Bible condemns the actice of bribery *(Isaiah 23)*.

Bribery often happens today.

Were Paul's Pockets Empty?

Was Felix stupid to try to get a bribe from a oor missionary?

Maybe not. Paul may not have had much noney, but he had many Christian friends, and everal of them were wealthy. Paul could have alled on them for money to pay Felix.

Rhyme Time

Complete these rhymes from this story.
1. About Christians Felix held his own views,
   But he was under pressure from the

   _____ .

2. Counting his losses and his gains,
   Felix left poor Paul in _____ .

3. He wanted to look calm; he really tried.
   But inside, Felix was _____ .

Answers: 1. Jews 2. Chains 3. Terrified

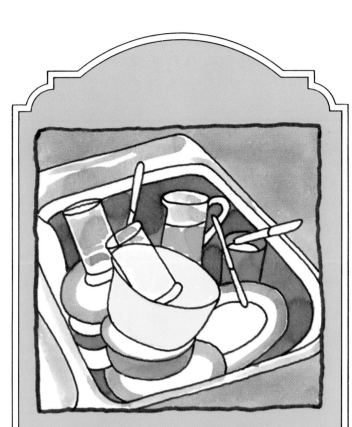

What Does This Mean to You?

Tomorrow, Tomorrow

Procrastinate is a word that describes what we all do to some extent. It means to put something off until tomorrow.

We put off hanging up our clothes. We let the dishes sit, in hopes that a little earthquake will come along that just destroys glasses and plates. We allow homework to wait until after our tv show, and then wonder why we can't understand fourteenth-century history. We put off saying things like "Thank you" and "I love you."

Some of us do this so often we have become professional procrastinators!

It makes much more sense to keep things up-to-date, and especially to keep close contact with our friends, our families, and God. If you put matters off, as Felix put off considering Jesus, you may run out of tomorrows.

Ticket to Rome
Acts 25: 9-12; 27: 1-8

9 Then Festus, anxious to please the Jews, asked Paul, "Are you willing to go to Jerusalem and stand trial before me?"

10, 11 But Paul replied, "No! I demand my privilege of a hearing before the emperor himself. You know very well I am not guilty. If I have done something worthy of death, I don't refuse to die! But if I am innocent, neither you nor anyone else has a right to turn me over to these men to kill me. I appeal to Caesar."

12 Festus conferred with his advisors and then replied, "Very well! You have appealed to Caesar, and to Caesar you shall go! . . ."

27 ARRANGEMENTS WERE FINALLY made to start us on our way to Rome by ship; so Paul and several other prisoners were placed in the custody of an officer named Julius, a member of the imperial guard.

2 We left on a boat bound for Greece,[1] which was scheduled to make several stops along the Turkish coast. . . .[2]

3 The next day when we docked at Sidon, Julius was very kind to Paul and let him go ashore to visit with friends and receive their hospitality.

4 Putting to sea from there, we encountered headwinds that made it difficult to keep the ship on course, so we sailed north of Cyprus between the island and the mainland,[3]

5 And passed along the coast of the provinces of Cilicia and Pamphylia, landing at Myra, in the province of Lycia.

6 There our officer found Egyptian ship from Alexandria bound for Italy, and put us aboard.

7, 8 We had several days rough sailing, and finally near Cnidus;[4] but the winds had become too strong, so we ran across to Crete, passing the por Salmone. Beating into the wir with great difficulty and movir slowly along the southern coa we arrived at Fair Havens, ne the city of Lasea.

[1]Literally, "Adramyttium," a Greek port.
[2]Literally, "the coast of Asia."
[3]Implied. Literally, "we sailed under the lee of Cyprus." Narr from that period interpret this as meaning what is indicated paraphrase above.
[4]Cnidus was a port on the southeast coast of Turkey.

Let's Pretend

What if Paul had taken advantage of Julius's friendship and escaped? The officer was taking a terrible risk by being kind to his prisoner.

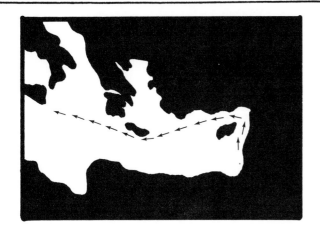

The Long Way Around

Why did an Egyptian ship go this route to Rome? It was risky to travel straight across the Mediterranean Sea. Strong winds came up quickly and could threaten the vessel's safety.

The ship hugged the shore closely until it reached Myra. Then it tried open sea. But the winds were so bad the ship sailed south for protection, around the island of Crete.

A Large Ship

The Egyptian vessel Paul rode in was huge. It was packed with grain, and also carried 276 passengers. The ship was powered by large sails.

Super Athletes?

The Bible says the apostle and friends *ran* across the water to Crete (verses 7, 8).

Their golf game wasn't bad. They *putted* all the way to the sea (verse 4).

All of this physical activity might be the reason why they stopped to see the "doc" at Sidon (verse 3).

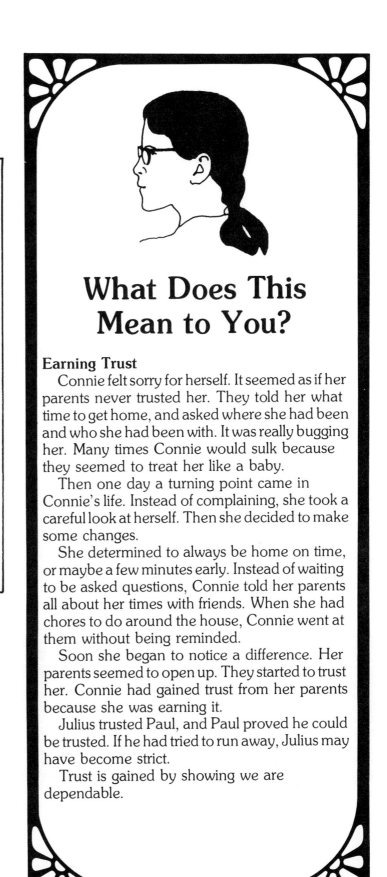

What Does This Mean to You?

Earning Trust

Connie felt sorry for herself. It seemed as if her parents never trusted her. They told her what time to get home, and asked where she had been and who she had been with. It was really bugging her. Many times Connie would sulk because they seemed to treat her like a baby.

Then one day a turning point came in Connie's life. Instead of complaining, she took a careful look at herself. Then she decided to make some changes.

She determined to always be home on time, or maybe a few minutes early. Instead of waiting to be asked questions, Connie told her parents all about her times with friends. When she had chores to do around the house, Connie went at them without being reminded.

Soon she began to notice a difference. Her parents seemed to open up. They started to trust her. Connie had gained trust from her parents because she was earning it.

Julius trusted Paul, and Paul proved he could be trusted. If he had tried to run away, Julius may have become strict.

Trust is gained by showing we are dependable.

Typhoon!

Acts 27: 14, 15, 18-32

14, 15 Shortly afterwards, the weather changed abruptly and a heavy wind of typhoon strength (a "northeaster," they called it) caught the ship and blew it out to sea. They tried at first to face back to shore but couldn't, so they gave up and let the ship run before the gale. . . .

18 The next day as the seas grew higher, the crew began throwing the cargo overboard.

19 The following day they threw out the tackle and anything else they could lay their hands on.

20 The terrible storm raged unabated many days,[1] until at last all hope was gone.

21 No one had eaten for a long time, but finally Paul called the crew together and said, "Men, you should have listened to me in the first place and not left Fair Havens—you would have avoided all this injury and loss!

22 "But cheer up! Not one of us will lose our lives, even though the ship will go down.

23 "For last night an angel of the God to whom I belong and whom I serve stood beside me,

24 "And said, 'Don't be afraid, Paul—for you will surely stand trial before Caesar! What's more, God has granted your request and will save the lives of all those sailing with you.'

25 "So take courage! For I believe God! It will be just as he said!

26 "But we will be shipwrecked on an island."

27 About midnight on the 14th night of the storm, as we were being driven to and fro on the Adriatic Sea, the sailors suspected land was near.

28 They sounded, and found 120 feet of water below them. A little later they sounded again, and found only 90 feet.

29 At this rate they knew they would soon be driven ashore; and fearing rocks along the coast, they threw out four anchors from the stern and prayed for daylight.

30 Some of the sailors planned to abandon the ship, and lowered the emergency boat as though they were going to put out anchors from the prow.

31 But Paul said to the soldiers and commanding officer, "You will all die unless everyone stays aboard."

32 So the soldiers cut the ropes and let the boat fall off.

[1] Literally, "neither sun nor stars shone upon us."

Thunder and Lightning

The storm hit with such force that the ship could not hold its course. The sailors were forced to give up and merely let it go out to sea as the wind pushed (*Acts 27:14, 15*).

The ship was driven for 480 miles in open, raging waters.

Feast for Fat Fish

Convinced they were all about to drown, the sailors threw all the cargo overboard. Their main cargo was grain from Egypt. When the storm died down, there must have been plenty of fat fish swimming around.

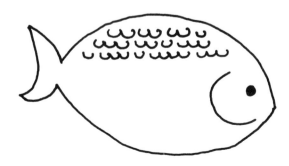

Change in Menu

The next day a different kind of supplies were thrown overboard. Any extra sails, crates, or hammers were tossed over. This must have been bewildering to the tiny sea creatures.

A Sick Ship

What was it like to suffer in a storm for this long? Try to imagine living with these problems:
- No food for fourteen days.
- Violent rocking of the ship.
- Wet clothes and bedding day and night.
- Fear that the next wave will break the ship in half.
- Little ability to see because of dark skies.

Testing, Testing

Sounding is a boating term meaning to measure the depth of the water. Weights were tied to a rope and lowered in the sea until they reached bottom. The wet part of the rope was then measured.

A sailor stretched the rope from one fingertip to the fingertip of the other hand. Each stretch was called a fathom, around six feet. The sailors first found themselves in twenty fathoms of water, and then in only fifteen fathoms.

Other ship terms: The *stern* is the back of a boat. The *prow*, or *bow*, is the front.

Next Time He'll Take the Train

If there had been trains in the first century, Paul would probably have taken one to Rome. This was one of at least three shipwrecks he was in *(2 Corinthians 11:25)*. He must have gotten tired of sitting in a soggy tunic and wet sandals.

Captain Paul

Paul had real leadership ability. He had boarded the ship as a lowly prisoner. But when danger struck, the apostle was soon giving instructions, and everyone obeyed.

Tension Time

Some sailors decided to try to make it to shore alone. They started to lower a small boat while pretending to carry an anchor out further from the ship.

Paul saw them, and the soldiers cut the ropes holding the boat so no one would leave. This could have led easily to a mutiny among the sailors and chaos on board.

Busy People

The sailors were busy acting and thinking. Can you match their thoughts and actions with the story? You might want to reread the story before answering.

1. They *threw* what overboard?
2. They *suspected* what?
3. What did they *fear*?
4. What did they *plan*?
5. What did they *pretend*?

Answers:
1. Cargo and tackle. 2. Land was near. 3. Rocks along the coast. 4. Abandon ship. 5. To put out anchors from the prow.

Riddle

Q. How do we know there was going to be music on board with Paul?

A. Verse 30 says the sailors planned a band on the ship.

What Does This Mean to You?

When Disaster Strikes

Have you ever wondered how you would behave if something terrible was happening? How you'd feel if you were in a tornado or a flood or a severe earthquake? We've all seen enough of such disasters on television to make us wonder how we'd react to facing injury or death.

I can't say that all Christians are automatically cool as cucumbers in such situations. Nor do we all come out like heroes. But as a Christian, you do have a few advantages over a non-Christian in a crisis.

First, you believe in a God who knows everything. He knows all that's happening to you, and you can pray to him when you're in trouble.

You believe in a God who is powerful. You know that God can rescue believers from terrible situations when he feels it is best.

Best of all, you believe in a God who cares about you, and has a plan for your life. You can grasp onto the knowledge that, whatever happens to you, God will work it out for your good and his glory. You can hang onto that knowledge and hope just like you'd hang onto a life preserver in a stormy sea.

Some of the sailors on Paul's ship panicked because of the storm. Paul could have panicked, too. But instead he was able to trust God and encourage the others around him.

The Shipwreck
Acts 27:33-36, 39-44

118

33 As the darkness gave way to the early morning light, Paul begged everyone to eat. "You haven't touched food for two weeks," he said.

34 "Please eat something now for your own good! For not a hair of your heads shall perish!"

35 Then he took some hardtack and gave thanks to God before them all, and broke off a piece and ate it.

36 Suddenly everyone felt better and began eating. . . .

39 When it was day, they didn't recognize the coastline, but noticed a bay with a beach and wondered whether they could get between the rocks and be driven up onto the beach.

40 They finally decided to try. Cutting off the anchors and leaving them in the sea, they lowered the rudders, raised the foresails and headed ashore.

41 But the ship hit a sandbar[1] and ran aground. The bow of the ship stuck fast, while the stern was exposed to the violence of the waves and began to break apart.

42 The soldiers advised their commanding officer to let them kill the prisoners lest any of them swim ashore and escape.

43 But Julius[2] wanted to spare Paul, so he told them no. Then he ordered all who could swim to jump overboard and make for land,

44 And the rest to try for it on planks and debris from the broken ship. So everyone escaped safely ashore!

[1]Literally, "a place where two seas met."
[2]Implied.

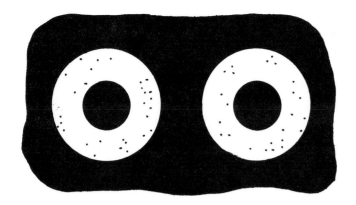

Break out the Cheerios

While others were near panic, Paul thought about food. He knew everyone would be safe. Paul was cool because he believed what God had promised.

When the passengers were able to eat breakfast they started to feel better. Simple things like eating regularly make the tough things of life easier for our bodies and emotions to handle.

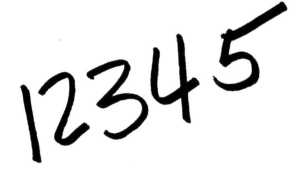

Take Your Turn

In the middle of the storm, Paul prayed and gave thanks to God.

You have probably never been in a shipwreck situation, but you still have plenty to be cheerful about. Quickly name five things you can thank God for.

Emergency Measures

Preparing for disaster, the crew took several steps to make the ship easier to manage.
- They cut off the anchors.
- Paddles were lowered to guide the vessel.
- A small sail was raised to give some control to the craft.

Stuck in the Muck

The bow of the ship rammed into a sandbar and stuck there. Its stern was left free to be beaten by the storm. The wind was so violent that the ship began to split apart.

Out of Chains

During the storm, the prisoners had probably been let out of their chains. Now the soldiers were concerned that the prisoners would get away. The soldiers would have been held responsible for such an escape *(Acts 12:19)*.

Julius to the Rescue

The commander had been kind to Paul throughout the trip *(verse 3)*. He was not about to allow Paul to be killed.

No Life Jackets

Swimming, floating on planks, possibly holding clothes filled with air, grabbing anything that would keep them up, the sailors, soldiers, and prisoners struggled to shore. *Miraculously, not one person lost his life.*

What Does This Mean to You?

Happiness Germs

Have you ever noticed how you affect other people in your house? If you bounce into the living room after school saying nice things, the family seems to perk up. On the other hand, when you plop down at the table, griping into your macaroni, you throw ice water on everyone's mood.

You have a lot of control over others. That gives you a great opportunity to put happiness into someone else's life.

Paul was in the middle of a sad, hopeless group. Everything looked gloomy to them. Yet one person's cheer, one person's happiness, and one person's faith turned a shipload of attitudes around.

Smiles are contagious. When you show them to others, they begin to spread. We happy Christians have some good germs to share!

The Case of the Venomous Viper
Acts 28:1-10

28 WE SOON LEARNED that we were on the island of Malta.

2 The people of the island were very kind to us, building bonfire on the beach to welcom and warm us in the rain and col

3 As Paul gathered an armf of sticks to lay on the fire, a poisonous snake, driven out b the heat, fastened itself onto h hand!

4 The people of the island saw it hanging there and said each other, "A murderer, no doubt! Though he escaped the sea, justice will not permit him live!"

5 But Paul shook off the snake into the fire and was unharmed.

6 The people waited for hi to begin swelling or suddenly fa dead; but when they had waited long time and no harm came t him, they changed their minds and decided he was a god.

7 Near the shore where we landed was an estate belonging t Publius, the governor of the island. He welcomed us courteously and fed us for thre days.

8 As it happened, Publius's father was ill with fever and dysentery. Paul went in and prayed for him, and laying his hands on him, healed him!

9 Then all the other sick people in the island came and were cured.

10 As a result we were showered with gifts,[1] and when the time came to sail, people pu on board all sorts of things we would need for the trip.

[1]Literally, "honors."

Goon Today, God Tomorrow

Residents of Malta allowed circumstances to rule their minds. First they thought Paul was a criminal. When he did not die from snakebite, they decided he must be a god.

A Silly Superstition

The unbelievers on the island thought the snakebite was sure evidence that Paul was evil. People have often believed the nonsense that all accidents and disasters come as punishment from God.

It's not true. A stolen bicycle is not to be understood as a judgment of God on you. A day with the flu does not mean you have disobeyed God.

Paul's Personality

The apostle had just been through a long, terrible ordeal. However, soon after he was safely on land, Paul was gathering firewood. Unwilling to be waited on, he jumped in and helped.

A Medical Missionary

Paul knew the governor's father was terribly uncomfortable. He was hot with a fever. His dysentery meant that he had to make a lot of trips to the bathroom.

A caring man, Paul could demonstrate his love for people's bodies as well as people's souls. Many medical missionaries have gone out over the centuries with the same caring spirit.

Rebus Quiz

What is happening to Paul?

Answer: Paul is being showered with gifts.

What Does This Mean to You?

Emergency Energy

After Arnold's heart attack, he tried to avoid picking up anything heavy. The doctor said it was risky to have much strain.

But one day Arnold saw a five-year-old boy playing in some cast iron pipes. An 18-foot-long pipe rolled and the boy tumbled under it. The pipe, weighing 1800 pounds, rested on the trapped boy's head.

Without giving his heart problems a thought, Arnold ran over and lifted the pipe. As he held it up, some girls pulled the little boy free.

Later Arnold went back to try to pick up the pipe. He could not lift it, and neither could anyone else in the crowd that gathered. Arnold may have been helped by a hormone called adrenaline, which the body can produce for extra strength in times of emergency.

God offers you mental and emotional adrenaline. Sometimes you may not feel like sharing yourself and your energy, but deep down inside you know that is the loving thing to do. God can help if you ask him.

Rome at Last!
Acts 28:11, 15-17, 21-24, 30, 31

11 It was three months after the shipwreck before we set sail again, and this time it was in "The Twin Brothers" of Alexandria, a ship that had wintered at the island. . . .

15 The brothers in Rome had heard we were coming and came to meet us at the Forum on the Appian Way. Others joined us at The Three Taverns. When Paul saw them he thanked God and took courage.

16 When we arrived in Rome, Paul was permitted to live wherever he wanted to, though guarded by a soldier.

17 Three days after his arrival, he called together the local Jewish leaders and spoke to them as follows: "Brothers, I was arrested by the Jews in Jerusalem and handed over to the Roman government for prosecution, even though I had harmed no one nor violated the customs of our ancestors. . . ."

21 They replied, "We have heard nothing against you! We have had no letters from Judea or reports from those arriving from Jerusalem.[1]

22 "But we want to hear what you believe, for the only thing we know about these Christians is that they are denounced everywhere!"

23 So a time was set and on that day large numbers came t his house. He told them about th Kingdom of God and taught the about Jesus from the Scriptures from the five books of Moses ar the books of prophecy. He bega lecturing in the morning and we on into the evening!

24 Some believed, and son didn't. . . .

30 Paul lived for the next tw years in his rented house[2] and welcomed all who visited him,

31 Telling them with all boldness about the Kingdom c God and about the Lord Jesu Christ; and no one tried to sto him.

[1]Implied.

[2]Or, "at his own expense."

Rest and Recreation

More than one ship was forced to find shelter at Malta. *The Twin Brothers,* a ship from Alexandria, spent three months in port there. The 276 people from Paul's ship boarded *The Twin Brothers.* They probably left for Rome in early February.

A Superhighway

The Appian Way was the first of Rome's paved highways. It was built so well that cars can travel on some of the original paving today—yet the Romans began constructing it three hundred years before Christ!

Christians from Rome traveled about forty miles south of the city to see Paul at Forum of Appius. Appius was a market town on the Appian Way. The Three Taverns was a few miles closer to Rome.

No Telephones

Some time before, Paul had written the Epistle to the Romans to the Christians in Rome. He was now going to meet them for the first time.

News moved rapidly in the first century. The Christians somehow knew Paul had landed in Italy, and made arrangements to meet him. Perhaps they had heard about his arrival from someone on another ship out of Malta.

Time Flies

Twenty-five years after the resurrection of Jesus Christ, his message had spread widely. A church now existed in faraway Rome, and many people had heard of this faith.

House Prisoner

Paul remained a prisoner in Rome for two years. While there he lived in his own rented home, guarded by a soldier, and paid his own expenses.

Where did he get the money? He may have been allowed to work—possibly making tents. Or Christian friends may have supported the apostle.

A Quick Quiz

1. Name the ship Paul boarded at Malta.
2. Which Scriptures did Paul use?
3. What was the reaction to Paul's teaching?
4. How long did Paul live in Rome?
5. Where did Paul live in Rome?

Answers:
1. The Twin Brothers.   2. Five books of Moses and the books of prophecy.   3. Some believed and some didn't.   4. Two years.   5. His own rented house.

125

What Happened to Paul?

The Book of Acts ends without finishing Paul's story. We don't know exactly what happened in the rest of his life, but the letters he wrote to churches give us some clues, and so does ancient church tradition.

1. After his two years of house arrest, Paul was apparently set free, and did some more traveling and preaching. Perhaps his enemies did not show up at his trial to press charges. Or perhaps a judge found him innocent.

2. After several years, Paul was arrested and taken to Rome a second time. This time he was chained in a real prison (2 Timothy 2:9). He had another trial, and felt that God saved him from being thrown to the lions (2 Timothy 4:17).

3. Tradition says that Paul was finally beheaded by the crazy Roman emperor, Nero. Paul had written his feelings about death down sometime earlier in a letter: "For me, living means opportunities for Christ, and dying—well, that's better yet! . . . I long to go and be with Christ. . . . but I am still needed down here" (Philippians 1:21, 23, 25).

What About Peter?

Bible evidence seems to show that after the church council in Acts 15 (the "free gift" chapter), Peter turned over the leadership of the Jerusalem church to James (Acts 21:18). Then Peter seems to have gone on missionary trips, as Paul had. The Bible contains letters from him to areas he apparently visited (1 and 2 Peter).

The first of Peter's letters seems to have been written from Rome (1 Peter 5:13), so Peter and Paul may have been together there. Ancient church tradition says that Peter, like Paul, was executed by Nero.

What Does This Mean to You?

God Is Full of Surprises

When you began studying the Book of Acts, you probably never would have guessed that the handful of confused and lonely believers who saw Christ rise into the sky could spread Christ's message to thousands of people.

When you first read about Paul and his anger at Christians, you probably never would have guessed that he would carry Christianity all the way to the capital of the Roman Empire.

They did it! They were beaten, arrested, stoned, shipwrecked, executed, and hated, but they did it. Courageous Christians took the story of Jesus Christ around the world.

Because of their sacrifices, the Good News has found its way into our times and into our lives. We can believe in Jesus. We can know the love of the Son of God. We can serve him.

You might not believe it, but God can use you to spread his Good News—starting right now. You can thank God for courageous Christians—and you can be one yourself.